PRAISE FOR *SUICIDE JOCKEYS*

"This inspiring story of the long-forgotten World War II glider program is a great read. Monique Taylor lays out these incredible events as only a loving daughter can do, from the heart! Her father, and the rest of the glider pilots, were caught between two worlds, not considered to be a part of the real Army Air Force and not trained to fight as infantry, even after landing behind enemy lines. To end the critical four-day battle at La Fiere bridge, General Gavin called on the glider infantry troops to conduct an assault once again, across the bridge. The victory on that causeway and the delivery of 57 mm anti-tanks guns via glider, saved Ste.-Mere-Eglise and reinforced the success of our brave paratroopers from two airborne divisions. The glider troops and the pilots who flew them will remain a part of airborne history for as long as the US Army exists.

"These pilots were a vital part of the greatest generation, and Monique Taylor reminds us that our obligation is to never forget their sacrifice. Glider pilots flew and fought not to conquer nations but to provide freedom to oppressed people. Well done!"

—Mike Thornton, Colonel, US Army (Ret.), Loudon, Tennessee

"Without doubt, the overall organization and implementation of the glider program is exceptionally addressed. I was particularly drawn to the operational parts of the book. Various combat missions are addressed with vivid descriptions, described in detail and supported by the actual pilot's (individual names included) description from his own written interrogation report—the report he has written immediately following the mission. These reports are very specific and tend to place the reader right at the scene, almost like an eyewitness.

"This is an outstanding work, identifying pilots and soldiers by name, highlighting major developments, events, locations, and conclusions. The author's intent is fully satisfied, while adding comprehensive documentation to the present limited glider program information."

—James C. Pollard, Lieutenant Colonel (Ret.), US Army, Former Paratrooper

"I have always enjoyed reading about the smaller details about military history. I thoroughly enjoyed reading about the glider pilots of WWII. My first duty assignment was to a former glider infantry regiment, the 327th Infantry Regiment of the 101st ABN Div. Having a small knowledge base about them, I felt this book gives a great insight to a novice historian about a dangerous and less-talked-about job during World War II. It is great to see a different perspective of D-Day through the eyes of glider pilots. Thank you for your contribution to keeping history alive."

—Gabriel A. Candelaria, Master Sergeant, Senior Military Science Instructor, Military History Instructor, University of Texas

"Cornelius Ryan's books, autobiographies of the likes of Ridgway, Gavin, Taylor, and so on, focus on paratroopers and the airborne as some of the most elite troops of WWII, and deservingly so. But all too often overlooked, understated, or underappreciated is the role played by a handful of men who performed extraordinary feats, at considerable risk, and without which the airborne forces could not have fought as they did. Their story has been told before, but benefits from being retold and emphasized."

—Leonard J. Fullenkamp, Colonel (Ret.), US Army

"OUTSTANDING! Monique Taylor tells the incredible story of the US Army WWII glider program with the soul of a researcher, the mind of a historian, and the heart of a daughter. She captures the most important aspects of this little-known program, beginning with its inception. She fills the pages with incredible amounts of data, references, and firsthand accounts of these incredibly brave young men who had little knowledge of what they were about to experience in the hell of WWII. Her father, glider pilot Lt. Col. Paul W. Mousseau Sr., would be very proud of the work Monique put into this book, as am I."

—Gary Stripling, Chair and Research Team Manager, National WWII Glider Pilots Association

"A succinct and profoundly accurate description of a glider pilot comes near the end of Monique Taylor's highly informative and equally entertaining book, *Suicide Jockeys: The Making of the WWII Combat Glider Pilot*. It's Gen. William Westmoreland that Taylor quotes, writing that they were 'intrepid pilots . . . whose duty it was to deliberately crash land, and then go on to fight as combat infantrymen.' I'd wager most historians and students of the Second World War and avid readers of military literature know little about the thousands of young men who took to the skies on one-way missions in craft made of plywood, fabric, and glue to deliver men and materiel to the battlefield. To fill the knowledge gap, and to bring long overdue recognition to these extraordinary aviators, Taylor combed through military archives, read countless wartime reports, and conducted firsthand interviews with experts in the field. Then, she deftly interwove her narrative with anecdotes that sit the reader on that thin plywood seat as the glider approaches the earth soundlessly and in the black of night. Hold on tight, dear reader, for a fabulous ride with these unsung heroes!"

—Rona Simmons, Author of *A Gathering of Men* and *The Other Veterans of World War II*

"The daughter of a WWII glider pilot and a college-level history professor for twenty years, there is nobody more suited to write the story of the making and training of WWII glider pilots than Monique Taylor. Painstakingly researched and documented, her book *Suicide Jockeys: The Making of the WWII Combat Glider Pilots* will not only fill a critical void in WWII USAAF history but will also highlight the bravery of these unsung heroes. The 'G' on their wings stood for 'guts,' as it took a lot of guts to fly unarmored and unarmed gliders low and slow to landings behind enemy-held lines. Gliders brought combat infantrymen, jeeps, artillery, ammunition and medical supplies to the battlefield and were a lifeline to airborne units until they could link up with ground forces. This book is a must-read and is a fine addition to any library for anybody interested in WWII airborne troop carrier and glider operations."

—Mark C. Vlahos, Colonel (Ret.), USAF, WWII Historian, Author and Speaker

"This new study of the WWII glider program, and the pilots who flew the gliders, is a welcome addition to the sparse history of the little-known program and its even lesser-known pilots. *Suicide Jockeys* is a focused study, written to address the most confusing and controversial aspects of the gliders in WWII. The author deals with three basic issues: the ill-defined role of the pilots in combat, the confusing and oft changed training program, and the overall day-to-day structure and operations of the troop carrier groups scattered around the world. While most books deal with the chronological history and military operations of the gliders, few even touch on these three issues and certainly do not delve into them in any depth. Monique Taylor provides a great service to those interested in the glider program, by explaining these three most overlooked and misunderstood aspects of the glider program. Suicide Jockeys is a must-have for those reading and/or writing about the WWII glider program."

—Don Abbe, National WWII Glider Pilots Association, Author, Liaison, Silent Wings Museum

"After reading *Suicide Jockeys: The Making of the WWII Combat Glider Pilot*, I have a new appreciation of the role of the glider pilots. I honestly did not realize how significant their role was. I found myself getting angry, sympathetic, and respectful of their role. No one certainly had it easy, but I think the glider pilots did double duty. There were many unsung heroes in the war, but especially those glider pilots who stepped forward despite the odds against them that brings them to the top of the bar."

—P. Brown, WWII Enthusiast, Son of WWII 11th Infantry Airborne Paratrooper

"Monique's *Suicide Jockey* has left no stone unturned with a masterful blend of detailed research and firsthand accounts. You can sense the passion to carry on the story of the warriors who were the 'boys in the CG-4As.' The author not only creates an atmosphere of empathy towards the chaotic nature of the glider pilot program but also tastefully captures the reality of wartime. When looking at the entire picture, one can only agree—these men's stories are distinctly unique and must be shared!"

—Joshua Mousseau, Reader

"*Suicide Jockeys* is the history lesson that I never knew I wanted to learn about. I have read a lot about WWII and had never heard of the glider pilots. This book is a great tribute to these brave men who served our country. Those men were thrown into volatile situations without the proper training necessary at times, which speaks of the desperation during the war years. Their contribution to several wars was all but lost, barely recorded. This book provides in-depth details and even brutally honest firsthand accounts of the trials and tribulations that these pilots endured. It is a must-read for anyone who has a thirst for knowledge relating to the wars during the 1940s. A truly informative read."

—Lori Bramlett, Reader

"You do not have to be a historian to find interest in the unknown story of the WWII combat glider pilots. The glider pilots were part of the greatest generation whose sacrifices should never be forgotten. My grandfather was a glider pilot. Thank you for taking the stories we heard growing up and writing a book so this group of unknown war heroes could be recognized."

—A. Fogleman, Reader

"This book was very different than I'm used to, but what I loved about it were the actual facts mixed with original sources from the glider pilot mission reports. This gave insight into what the glider pilots went through. Whenever I read books of this genre, I have such a new appreciation of how many men like your dad and this group of combat gliders sacrificed for the greater good. I feel that history teachers/classes would get more out of a book like this than the regular history books. I also have such gratitude to authors like you who take the time and energy to get stories like this out there, so they will never be forgotten. I will make sure our book club knows about this, and when it's my month to pick one, I hope this is what we read. Thanks for sharing this with me."

—Madelon Madeley, Reader

"Where have these stories been? To just now be learning about these men and their harrowing experiences has left me speechless. These men literally risked their lives on every single mission. Piloting a plane has its own dangers; piloting a plane with no engine has a whole other set of issues; and lastly, piloting a plane with no engine into enemy territory is like skinny-dipping in a school of sharks. The fact that so many men volunteered for this is unbelievable. At times they lacked training, supplies, and support, and still they performed one of the most dangerous jobs in the military. In my humble opinion, these men were the real unsung heroes. Why hasn't Hollywood made a movie about this yet?"

—Nancy Todd, Reader

Suicide Jockeys: The Making of the WWII Combat Glider Pilot
by Monique Taylor

© Copyright 2023 Monique Taylor

ISBN 979-8-88824-144-8

All rights reserved. No part of this publication may be reproduced, stored in a retrieval system, or transmitted in any form or by any means—electronic, mechanical, photocopy, recording, or any other—except for brief quotations in printed reviews, without the prior written permission of the author.

Published by

◤köehlerbooks™

3705 Shore Drive
Virginia Beach, VA 23455
800-435-4811
www.koehlerbooks.com

SUICIDE JOCKEYS

THE MAKING OF THE WWII COMBAT GLIDER PILOT

MONIQUE TAYLOR

VIRGINIA BEACH
CAPE CHARLES

To my father,
the bravest man I know.

TABLE OF CONTENTS

Preface xiii
Introduction xix

Chapter 1: The Setting 1
1.1 Allied Glider Operations of WWII 3

Chapter 2: Silent Flight 12
2.1 The Glider 15
2.2 Method of Operation 22
2.3 The Pilot 39

Chapter 3: The Evolution of the Glider Pilot 55
3.1 Recruitment 57
3.2 Combat Training 67
3.3 Rank 75

Chapter 4: Troop Carrier 83
4.1 Duties 85
4.2 Pre-Mission Training and Briefings 92
4.3 Evacuation 98
4.4 Equipment 105

Chapter 5: Combat 115
5.1 In Combat 115
5.2 The 3 B's 125
5.3 Commendations 128

Acknowledgments *134*
Selected Bibliography *136*
Appendix A: USAAF Ranks During World War II *145*
Appendix B: Flow of Students Through Glider Schools *146*

AUTHOR'S NOTE

The quoted material and entries enclosed have not been edited per the *Chicago Manual of Style* to maintain the authenticity of the singular experiences being reported with all the accompanying stresses of recent combat. Citations for primary sources have followed the National Archives recommendation to cite in the form that will best allow researchers to find the records. I have added further information on the repositories holding the records in the bibliography. The original captions on the photographs have been added to or altered to highlight specific elements I wished to draw attention to.

PREFACE

"All of us in the 81st TCS, whatever our job, have strongly etched memories not only of gliders soaring in the sky but also of gliders lined up on the ground taking on airborne infantry; gliders being towed in formation; gliders in hangars, their holes being patched up with a piece of fabric and glue. Our glider pilots, however, have a different set of glider images: gliders horribly smashed up on a field of combat, gliders smeared along a stone wall or hedgerow, glider contents, including mangled bodies, strewn about the ground."

—Martin Wolfe, *Green Light*

The original title of this book was *The Boys in the CG-4As*, and in all rights, it is the correct title. The credit for such an accurate description of them belongs to one of their own, Flight Officer Issac E. Rhodes, a member of the 441st Troop Carrier Group (TCG), 99th Troop Carrier Squadron (TCS). During my research in completion of my master's thesis, I came across Flight Officer Rhodes's statement in an Air Intelligence Contact Unit interview.[1] It was the last line in a multipage document that stayed with me. His statement read, "We glider pilots feel that the people here in the United States don't appreciate the character of our operations, and it is hoped that when the history of operations in the ETO [European Theater of Operations] is written up, they will reserve a few pages for the

---

1 The Air Intelligence Contact Unit was based stateside and interviewed a number of glider pilots. They are not after action reports completed upon returning from a mission but instead are interviews on a number of subjects.

exploits of the boys in the CG-4As."² History did not reserve a few pages for them, it barely reserved a few sentences, and the saga of the World War II glider pilot is fast disappearing.

My other motivation for writing this was my father, Lt. Col. Paul W. Mousseau (USAF ret.). At seventeen years old, he entered the service as a private. When his sergeant asked if anyone had flying experience, he stepped forward, having had some private flying lessons. He was then called to the colonel's office, who congratulated him on becoming a glider pilot. He addressed my father as sergeant. My father corrected him, to which he received the reply, "I can take a sergeant and teach him to fly, or I can take a pilot and make him a sergeant, Sergeant!" and thus began my father's military career as a glider pilot in 1942. He somehow survived all his missions and quickly ascended the ranks during the war. After the war, the military became his career. Like many other glider pilots I came to meet, he was deeply disappointed that there was little interest in their contributions to the war. Then, like today, many people were not truly familiar with the glider pilot program. Yet the deaths of friends and fellow pilots that died completing the airborne mission was real to the men that flew the gliders and to the families that spent a lifetime mourning their losses.

Isaac Rhodes and Paul Mousseau were the two men that were and have been my primary motivators to publish this book. There is yet a third reason. The glider pilots' missions and contributions to the war have been largely neglected by historians since World War II. The important role they played and the invaluable service they gave, both of which helped make the operations they took part in a success, will soon be forgotten. With so many books written and films made about bomber and fighter pilots, tank troops, and paratroopers in WWII, this book is just a small voice in a gale about

---

2   F/O Issac Rhodes, *"Glider Operations in Southern France and Holland,"* Air Intelligence Combat Unit, AAF Redistribution Station No. 3, Santa Monica, California, 441st TCG, 99th TCS, 9th Air Force. May 15, 1945, 3.

a lesser known aviator in the war. But, just like the glider pilot needed to make each landing a good landing and walk away intact, one book and one reader that connect with the men in this story and carry it to others can change history when it is multiplied by hundreds. We can do what historians have neglected to do and make sure the glider pilots are given their rightful place in history. One they richly deserve, they earned it with blood, sweat, and serious injury or death.

In the end, I decided not to go with *The Boys in the CG-4As* as a title and instead went with *Suicide Jockeys*. The glider pilots used that moniker for themselves not as a badge of honor but more as a self-deprecatory statement of irony that, in many cases, summed up the role they felt they were given. Such sarcasm was not uncommon; the tow pilots often referred to the C-46 they piloted as "flaming coffins" due to its tendency to leak hydraulic fluid, the vapors of which could explode from a spark.[3] As for the "boys in the CG-4As," the difference is in the connotation of "boys," as if part of a gang in the 1940s, and today's connotation as an adolescent male is important. I don't know that the glider pilots considered themselves boys at the time and probably would have bridled at being called such by todays interpretation. My father, entering the service at seventeen, was a boy, and he was flying gliders shortly thereafter. He is now buried at Arlington Cemetery after he had the privilege of living to age eighty-eight. The young soldier buried next to him was eighteen. I am sure my father considers him a boy when it comes to their relative ages. Many of the boys in the CG-4As were boys in respect to their ages, but in terms of carrying out their duties, they were exceptional men.

A very brief explanation about the methodology used in my research is necessary here. First-person accounts, which are considered primary sources and thus "gold" for a professional historian, sometimes contradict one another. It is important to note that no one generalized statement or source captures the true

---

3 Martin Wolfe, *Green Light: Men of the 81st Troop Carrier Squadron Tell Their Story* (Philadelphia, Penn: University of Pennsylvania Press, 1989), 127.

essence of an experience. The same is true here; the issues discussed and the conclusions drawn are based on the primary resources I came across and used in researching and writing *Suicide Jockeys*, but that does not mean it was every glider pilot's or group's experience. However, when a large number of participants continue to cite the same experiences and/or issues, some conclusions can be drawn as to the causes and consequences of those collective experiences. One example is the misconceptions about the age, eyesight, skill, and abilities of the glider pilots that have become the norm rather than the possible exception; this has done considerable damage to the glider pilots' reputation since the end of WWII. In my research, I did not come upon any reports that mentioned issues with eyesight or age. I did find an incomplete report written in the China Burma India Theater (CBI) that stated many of the glider pilots in the Air Commandos fell in the overage group. This is a moving target since the age requirement changed a few times during the war, and to verify or deny this was the norm in the CBI without further research would be pure speculation on my part. However, in most instances, all of these experiences, beliefs, and opinions of the glider pilot and the program itself are true and, at the same time, not true.

The truth and accuracy about the glider pilots lie in the investigation and research of the glider pilot program. The glider pilot program and, consequently, the glider pilots were in a constant state of flux for the greater part of the war. Was the glider pilot solely an aviator or aviator and infantryman? Arguments were sound on both sides of the equation. However, the lack of consensus about the glider pilot's role between two arms of the Army Air Corps, namely the Army and the Air Forces, was reflected in the mismatch between the glider pilot's rank and leadership duties as well as his ground combat expectations and training. It is clear that the glider pilot program fell into a gap within the extremely dynamic environment of a major power conflict.

Suicide Jockeys: The Makings of the WWII Combat Glider Pilot is based primarily on my research into the official Glider Pilot Training Program, the glider pilots' role in combat, and the United States Army Air Force's part in that drama. It is important for anyone reading or writing about World War II to understand that there were no official Air Force historians until after the end of the war. Consequently, to a large extent, the saved documents were left to the prerogative of the individuals sorting and discarding paperwork. In some cases, entire contents of desks were wiped into boxes, sealed, and stored. One such example is a box from my research, which contained a combat boot and a note to a medic. According to the archivists at the National Archives, only 13 percent of the paperwork generated in WWII was saved. Therefore, we do not know what potential sources are missing.

The sources I relied upon included various versions of glider pilot interrogation check sheets and troop carrier mission report. These are the firsthand written narratives describing the action, conditions, and experiences of said operations fresh after the return of the tug crews, glider pilots, and copilots. Also consulted were reports and studies filed by the various commands and units in the Army Air Corps and United States Army Air Forces, and personal interviews with both glider and tow pilots. I have chosen to use the spelling and punctuation in the after-action reports without corrections or indications of misspellings to allow the character of individual participant and the stresses of combat to come through. As with any piece of research, copious amounts of reading also took place. The results clearly demonstrate the handicaps under which the glider pilot operated. After reading *Suicide Jockeys*, I think you will agree with me that, considering training and supplies, the glider pilot has become one of the most misunderstood, underappreciated figures in history and one of the most remarkable of men under pressure.

INTRODUCTION

The song of the German Pilots:
"The sun shines red, comrades there is no going back."
The motto of the British Glider Pilot Regiment:
"Nothing is impossible."
The battle cry of the American Glider Pilots:
"Jesus Christ! More spoilers!"[1]

—Milton Dank, *The Glider Gang*

To refer to the glider pilots as *Suicide Jockeys* is, in many ways, inaccurate. They weren't kamikaze pilots, they had no wish to die, and they didn't sign up to die. They signed up to serve their country, liberate people in other countries, and, if necessary, give their lives doing so. They recognized the dangers of what they had volunteered to do by becoming a glider pilot, albeit perhaps a bit after the fact; nonetheless, they did what the job required and were a major contributing factor to the war effort. This was no small feat, considering the obstacles the Army Air Corps (AAC)—soon to be reorganized into the United States Army Air Forces (AAF)—

---

1 For those that are not familiar with spoilers, here is an explanation: "Gliders use spoilers during their approach and landing. By extending spoilers, glider pilots can increase drag, lower the nose and descend faster without significantly increasing speed." Colin Cutter, "Wing Spoilers: How Destroying Lift Helps You Fly," Bold Method, May 7, 2015. https://www.boldmethod.com/learn-to-fly/aircraft-systems/wing-spoilers.

placed in their way.² The glider pilots bore the collateral damage of being caught in the power struggles between the two arms of the AAC/AAF: the commanders of the Army Ground Forces under the leadership of General Matthew Ridgeway, General James Gavin, and General Maxwell Taylor and the Air Forces under Commanding General of the Army Air Forces General Hap Arnold, a proponent of the combat glider, General James Dolittle, and General Carl Spaatz.

In general, the Air Force air commanders considered glider pilots to be pilots, although some felt they should not be equated with power pilots. In their view, the glider pilots' mission was complete once they landed behind enemy lines and made their way back to their assigned command post (CP) to be evacuated. This would free them up to fly additional missions if necessary. The Army commanders wanted the glider pilots to assume an infantry role upon landing, where they would fall under the control of the ground commanders who were ultimately responsible for all airborne forces on the ground. This alignment would have resembled British members of the Glider Pilot Regiment organization, whose glider pilots were trained to assume infantry upon landing and were part of the British airborne forces.

To the American ground commanders, unassigned forces

---

2   In February of 1942 "Executive Order 9082 Reorganizing the Army of the United States and Transfers of Functions within the War Department" was signed by President Franklin Roosevelt. It stated, in part, "the functions duties and powers of the commanding general, General Headquarters Air Force (Air Force Combat Command), and the Chief of the Air Corps are transferred to the commanding general Army Air Forces." This meant the AAC and the Combat Command no longer existed as separate entities. They became the United States Army Air Forces (USAAF/AAF) with General Hap Arnold as the commanding general. The Executive Order lasted for the duration of the war and was to extend for six months afterwards. By this Order the AAC ceased to stand as its own branch of Army Aviation as it had since 1926 and the Army Air Forces and Army Ground Forces were made co-equal commands in the USAAF. It was in this channel of friction between the two arms of the AAF the glider pilots found themselves. In brief: The AAC is not to be confused with the United States Army Air Forces formed in 1942, which is not to be confused with the with the United States Air Force (USAF), which resulted from the separation of the Army and the Air Force in 1947. Army Air Forces Historical Association, "Was it the Air Corps of the Army Air Forces in WWII," accessed November 2022, http://www.aafha.org/air-corps-or-air-forces.html.

without a clear mission, unaccompanied by the infantry training and equipment to carry out an assigned mission, were a liability. For the glider pilots, who were keenly aware they were considered the stepchildren of the Army Air Corps, they took their lives in their hands every time they flew into combat. This was borne out time and again from the inception of their training forward by the loss of their fellow glider pilots. It was only by the time of the last glider mission in the ETO, Operation Varsity, in 1945, that the glider pilots finally had support from both the Army and Air Force commands of the Army Air Forces. By that time, the later recruits to the program were fully trained for the dual scope of their missions, first a glider pilot and, once landed, as an infantry soldier. Those who did not receive the benefit of that full training had to learn by experience. The consequences of the inability of the forces within the AAF to come to an agreement until that time directly impacted the glider pilots' morale, training, support, equipment, and, ultimately, their lives.

The glider pilots comprised a small force conducting a relatively new form of warfare. World War II was the only time the major powers used the cargo glider in war. The relative number of glider pilots was a fraction of the number of individuals who took part in the conflict. Of the estimated 16.5 million Americans who served, approximately 6,000 to 7,000 were glider pilots.[3] The glider men made operations possible by delivering troops and cargo to the hottest battlefields. The gliders were flown directly in, often to enemy territory, with zero defensive capabilities and no way to gain altitude once released. There were no second chances for them or the airborne they transported. It was a one-way ticket to combat as the pilots were committed to landing regardless of the conditions and amount of enemy fire on the landing zones (LZ).

At the time of its inception, the glider pilot program was an

---

3   This is an estimate. The military called for 6,000 glider pilots at one point during the program's recruitment phase and 7,200 at another.

integral part of the newly implemented Allied Airborne Mission.[4] Flying and landing their engineless aircraft, the cargo glider, the glider pilots delivered massive quantities of men in the form of airborne infantry, a.k.a. "glider riders," medical personnel, supplies, ammunition, gasoline, weapons, jeeps, bulldozers, large artillery, and, in the CBI—mules—in carefully calculated and secured loads. The gliders landed in close proximity to one another, behind enemy lines and often right in the thick of action on their assigned landing zones, usually made up of small fields. Gliders did not need a landing strip and therefore had a decided advantage in that they could land where powered aircraft could not. By landing on landing zones behind an enemy line or near their objective, it allowed a fighting force and equipment to be assembled and ready for action almost immediately; if successful, this prevented the enemy from reacting in a timely manner. These forces, then, had the advantage of being supported by additional larger weapons, ammunition, gasoline, and transportation brought in by successive glider serials (waves of gliders).

In comparison to glider delivery of troops and equipment, the paratrooper who was dropped from the sky behind enemy lines could carry only a minimal amount of equipment on his body due to constraints of surface area, the weight of the equipment the individual carried, and the capabilities of his parachute. Larger weapons and artillery had to be dropped, sometimes in pieces, via parachute, but like the paratrooper, this limited the size of the equipment that could be dropped on or near a drop zone (DZ). A larger piece of equipment would need to be dropped in several pieces and reunited to be reassembled before use. The drops of men and cargo could be scattered over wide areas that delayed reorganization, resulting in the loss of men, weapons, and supplies, and it could subsequently directly affect actions where time was of the essence to maintain the

---

4   The term *"Airborne"* has been used in a number of ways as it evolved and led to some confusion as to what the term actually means. Airborne in WWII referred to the troops and equipment delivered to the battlefield by air via glider, parachute, or transport planes.

element of surprise.

Regardless of the existing rivalry between glider riders, glider pilots, and paratroopers, the paratroopers, amongst their other highly dangerous missions and objectives, were often dropped in advance of the glider landings to clear the landing zones of enemy troops so the gliders could land with their supplies and reinforcements. The highly trained paratroopers were not always assigned to clear the landing zones and were not always successful when they were, but they saved many lives in their efforts. They were an integral part in ensuring men and equipment arrived where and when it was needed. The expedited and organized delivery of critically needed cargo exponentially increased the glider riders and paratroopers' odds of success in battle and provided the crucial element of any long battle—the supply line. The loss or overextension of supply lines has been the downfall of many of the greatest armies in the history of the world. Tragically, battles also have heavy casualties and other men are needed to fill those gaps, to strengthen the lines or complete the mission. The airborne troops the glider pilots ferried, and often the glider pilots themselves, provided the manpower to fill those gaps.

Contrary to popular belief, gliders were not only utilized here or there; they were a powerful chess piece in the supporting effort of the main operational forces in all the major campaigns of World War II in the ETO and played a more limited but equally important role in the China Burma India Theater. Regardless of the theater of war, in every mission they conducted, they were a powerful and effective singular force. The amount of men and cargo they delivered was compounded by the number of serials that flew in. Often, successive waves of gliders arrived on the battlefields for days after the initial attack or, as in the case of Bastogne, after the initial action when the ground troops were virtually surrounded and in desperate need of supplies and medical personnel.

In terms of the resistance the gliders faced, the emphasis is often placed, and the accolades given, to the first serials of gliders that landed on the landing zones in an operation. That focus is misleading. The beauty of the gliders and their only defense was their silent arrival. Consequently, the enemy was not always waiting for the initial serials of gliders to land or knew where they were going to land. This was not true for the successive serials that were often met with fierce resistance, especially toward the end of the war when they faced increasingly desperate enemy troops. The enemy knew where they were landing, set up to do maximum damage to the men and equipment in the gliders, and often dug in and waited for them to arrive.

The United States did not introduce this novel form of warfare to the world. The Germans and Soviets initially had a decided advantage over the United States and Britain in airborne operations due to their continued development of the airborne concept between World Wars I and II. The Soviets were the first to perfect the use of airborne assault forces during this interlude. Conversely, the Allied powers allowed further possible development of the gliders to go by the wayside and saw no purposeful use of the glider in war. It was only at the start of WWII, when Germany used gliders in several smaller key assaults, that the Allies started paying attention to the tactical use of the German glider missions. The first was the successful attack on the Belgian Fort Eben Emael, where the Germans successfully conducted silent "spot" missions that could land troops or specialists in a specific area to avoid a long siege. The taking of the Fort opened the gateway to France and the staging point for attacks on Britain. In the German invasion of Crete, the Allies noted the German's combination of the glider's silent flight with distractors such as smoke to further hide their approach. The German glider pilots were then able to land small "concentrations" of unanticipated troops in unexpected areas, which caused confusion among the enemy. In Africa, the Allies paid attention to the German use of the glider for resupply missions to deliver a limited amount of vital supplies to the German forces and their further use of gliders to land saboteurs behind enemy lines.[5]

The German use of the glider ended early in the war. The last large-scale use of the German airborne was the invasion of Crete in May of 1941. During the deployment of the airborne in Crete, the Germans made mistakes, some of which the Allies learned from but initially repeated. The heavy casualties to the German glider troops in Crete, much like in the Allied invasion of Sicily, was caused by gliders and paratroopers being used as the initial assault wave, gliders being released too far from shore, a lack of suitable landing zones, and a failure to discern the location of the full defensive measures of the enemy. The German glider troops and paratroopers were spread very thinly across the island, many without effective weapons due to scattered drops and landings. One of multiple reasons for Hitler's ultimate success in Crete was due to the British decision not to destroy the landing strips. This allowed Germans to bring in larger planes with additional troops and larger, more powerful weapons, equipment, and supplies to overpower the Allies after hard fighting. The cost of this victory in terms of casualties, however, was very high, too high for Hitler. The Allies did not repeat this error.

The Allies learned in that mission what the Germans failed to; the tactical use of gliders with large numbers of glider infantry and paratroopers in unison was the weight that would tip the scale in an airborne invasion, and there was an additional need to carry in vital equipment in larger gliders. The Allies began to work diligently to design the cargo glider, striving for the glider that had a larger cargo capacity, was towable when fully loaded, and could land in limited spaces. This search, design, testing, production, transport of the glider, and use and training of the glider pilot all had to be done while fighting and supplying the larger war effort.

The development of the use of the glider ushered in the concept

---

5 Troop Carrier Division, Combat Operations Department, AAF School of Applied Tactics, "Technical Considerations in the Employment of the Military Glider," Major Kenneth Marts. *(201-4-8-L)*, Orlando Florida: AAF School of Applied Tactics, March 1944. 3.

referred to as "vertical employment" to "establish an airhead deep within enemy territory."[6] The glider allowed for the ability to insert troops by air within enemy territory and surround or envelop them to establish this airhead. This was the solution Hitler was looking for when he initially pursued the use of airborne forces to avoid the stalemate of trench warfare in World War I. Their well-planned and effective use allowed forces to leapfrog over the enemy line, so to speak. The Army Air Forces School at the Army Air Forces Center clearly understood the serious nature of the airborne mission they were developing. Lt. Col. Daniel Davidson wrote in *Airborne Army-Organization and Employment*, "While many airborne exploits may border on the sensational nevertheless, the true story of airborne tactics and strategy is a cold, deadly and serious business and calls for the most intensive training the army has to offer."[7] While he was referring specifically to the parachutists and glider troops, it can be argued that this would have included, by default, the glider pilots, who ferried the glider infantry in and often ended up fighting with them.

Just as quickly as the combat glider appeared on the scene, it disappeared. Between the end of WWII and the Korean War, the glider was eclipsed by the deployment of two major weapon systems: the C-119 aircraft and the helicopter. The C-119 was developed as a tactical transport aircraft that filled the United States Air Force's need for the airborne transport of men and equipment that would operate within a theater of operations.[8] It had the capacity to not only transport cargo up to 28,000 pounds, but rear clamshell doors allowed for the delivery of very large, heavy equipment by

---

6   Army Air Forces School AAF Center, "Airborne Army-Organization and Employment," Lt. Col. Daniel Danielson Inf., (200-4-84-L) (201-4-84-L), (600-4-84-L), Orlando, Florida: Ground and Navy Advisory Section, 1945. 1.
7   Army Air Force School, AAF "Airborne Army- Organization and Employment," 1.
8   National Security Act of 1947. 50 U.S.C. 3001, (1947). The National Security Act of 1947 followed Executive Order 9082 and established three separate and individual services: The Army, the Air Force, and the Navy, each with their own secretary, who reports to the civilian secretary of defense, who reports to the president, the commander in chief of the Armed Forces.

parachute rather than dismantling and carrying it in two gliders.[9] Larger cargo loads, such as vehicles, could not be dropped without the advancement of parachutes capable of delivering them safely to the ground. The G-11A parachute was developed around the same time and had a 5,000-pound maximum payload capacity.[10] Multiple parachutes could be attached to one load to corresponded with the weight of the item to be dropped. This new system also had its drawbacks: the cargo had to dropped at a higher altitude than the troops. If dropping both cargo and the troops a higher altitude had to be gained to drop the cargo, the plane then had to circle back at a lower altitude to drop the paratroopers.[11] The same issue of scattered troops and equipment that the use of gliders resolved remained. The further development and use of helicopters after WWII allowed men and supplies to be delivered in places where cargo planes could not land. This added an advantage over the glider; they could power themselves out of the area. The modern equivalent of this tactic is called "vertical envelopment," a type of mission conducted by a wide range of fixed, rotary, and tilt-rotor aircraft.[12]

---

9 "C-119 G," March Field Museum, accessed January 2023, https://www.marchfield.org/aircraft/cargo/c-119g-flying-boxcar-fairchild.
10 Aerospace America. "Meet the U.S. Army's New Parachute," March 1, 2020. https://aerospaceamerica.aiaa.org/departments/meet-the-u-s-armys-new-parachute/. Confirmed by Travis Aviation Museum April 2023.
11 Aerospace America. "Meet the U.S. Army's New Parachute," March 1, 2020. https://aerospaceamerica.aiaa.org/departments/meet-the-u-s-armys-new-parachute/. Confirmed by Travis Aviation Museum.
12 Captain Jonathon Taylor, MV-22B Osprey Pilot, U.S. Marine Corps, interview by author, April 12, 2023.

CHAPTER 1

THE SETTING

"Under most difficult conditions, including landing under fire in enemy occupied terrain, these glider pilots did a splendid job. On the ground they rendered most willing and effective service, providing local protection for the Division Command Post during the most critical period when the Division was under heavy attack from three sides.

Please express to all elements of your command who brought this Division in by glider or parachute, or who performed resupply missions for us, our admiration for their coolness under fire, for their determination to overcome all obstacles, and for their magnificent spirit of cooperation."

—General Ridgeway, Office of the Division Commander in the Field following the Normandy invasion.[1]

Since its inception during World War II, The American Glider Pilot Program has been the subject of controversy. Its glider pilots have been characterized as poorly trained, ill-disciplined soldiers, who were considered the bastards of the US Army Air Forces.[2] There are three very important interdependent factors at play here, which ultimately decided the quality of the soldier: 1) the bureaucratic proceedings, 2) military preparation, and 3) commendations.

---

1 Headquarters Airborne Division, Office of the Division Commander in the Field to commanding general, IX Troop Carrier Command, June 8, 1944.
2 Additional monikers for the glider pilots were Redheaded Stepchildren, Bastards of the Army Air Force, Those Damn Glider Pilots, and Suicide Jockeys.

Theoretically, the same bureaucracy that creates a military unit should formally define the expectations of its members. These definitions would, in turn, act as guidelines for setting the parameters of the training curriculums necessary to achieve the desired objectives in a soldier. Eventually, bureaucratic proceedings were responsible for the designation of rank, the level of which directly affected a soldier's ability to direct the actions of other individuals, as well as setting the social stratification within the units. In practice, the expectations of the glider pilots were never fully defined until the end of the war; this directly affected the training curriculum, especially in terms of combat training. Because these two basic tenets were never defined, there was no way to define—or achieve—the desired objective, which was ever-moving. This accounts for the multiple changes in the glider pilots ranks, which were altered as the upper commands struggled over what his role would be. If his role could not be decided, his need to command or follow and when could not be decided either. This left the glider pilot in a no-man's-land within their own Troop Carrier Groups, with no defined expectations other than to land on the landing zone and no organization, structure, or training to support anything other than flying a one-way trip, landing, and, for the most part, being left to their own devices afterward.

The second area of major importance was the soldier's military preparation for battle. The foundation and strength of his preparation depends on the quality and relevance of the training, the adherence to the doctrine of the instruction by the unit tasked with the training, and the ability of the individual soldier to be integrated into the forces tasked with completion of the combat mission. Upon this base, the final level of preparation was conducted prior to a mission. This included pre-mission practices and briefings, equipment issues, and planned evacuation procedures. The quality of these three factors appears to have most strongly influenced a soldier's morale and, ultimately, his performance. The glider pilot's preparation for battle was flight training and very limited combat training until later in the war. Their level of preparation through flight training was inconsistent initially, but eventually, it became streamlined. However, because of the failure to define the role and basic objectives of the glider pilot once he landed, his pre-mission briefings were, at times, not as complete as they felt they should be for the conditions they actually encountered, and both their equipment issues and evacuations suffered throughout the war.

Lastly, formal recognition either from military commanders or the public had a very profound effect on the individual soldier and the unit's morale. Formal recognition of the glider pilots was rare at best. Routine commendations were not the rule in the glider program, and frequent complaints from individuals cited a lack of recognition for a job well done; however, criticisms were freely given and common in terms of their organization within the group, their combat preparation, and the occupation after landing and evacuations. That the glider pilot morale suffered as a result is an understatement. The Army Air Forces inability to meet the first of these three criteria—defining the glider pilot's role and hence their objectives—had a cascading effect on the remaining criteria and placed the glider pilot in an untenable position in which his morale suffered greatly.

ALLIED GLIDER OPERATIONS OF WWII

As stated in the introduction, gliders were a powerful player in the supporting effort of the main operational forces in all the major campaigns of WWII. Specifically, they were used in eight major airborne operations in the ETO, beginning with the invasion of Sicily (Operation HUSKY) July 9, 1943, followed by the invasion of Normandy (Operation OVERLORD), June 6, 1944, the invasion of Southern France (Operation ANVIL /DRAGOON), August 15, 1944, the invasion of Holland (Operation MARKET-GARDEN),

September 17-27 1944, the resupply mission to encircled troops in BASTOGNE, December 26-January 1945, and crossing the Rhine in the last glider operation in the ETO (Operation VARSITY), March 24, 1945. Gliders also were used in China Burma India Theater (Operation THURSDAY), March 5, 1944.

The first of these major glider missions was the invasion of Sicily, Operation HUSKY, on July 9, 1943. It was the first combined British/American airborne operation whose objective was to wrest Sicily from the hands of the Axis powers. Foreseeably, high casualty rates resulted due to several factors, including wrestling over control of the airborne forces between the Allied powers, the troop carrier glider tow ship combinations being committed to the invasion despite a lack of adequate training, and the British glider pilots operating the American CG-4A with little training. The American glider pilots were responsible for the limited training the British had in the gliders prior to the operation and volunteered as copilots to fill the shortage of British glider pilots. The oversights were compounded by gale force winds, rough seas, complicated routes, overcast skies, reduced visibility, miscommunications, inoperable intercom systems between tow ship and glider, and early glider releases too far from shore. Tragically, many deaths were caused by friendly fire from naval ships.

Operation LADROKE was the code name given to the opening glider tow mission in Sicily. The mission involved 144 gliders—136 were CG-4As and 8 were British Horsa gliders. They were piloted by British glider pilots, with twenty-two American glider pilots who acted as copilots.[3] Six of the twenty-two American glider pilots were killed in action.[4] FUSTIAN, a combined glider tow and paratroop drop, was the second lift. FUSTIAN consisted of eight CG-4As and eleven British Horsa gliders. There were a total of thirty-eight British pilots, four of which were Americans acting as copilots taking part.[5]

---

3   Mark C. Vhalos, COL. USAF ret., *Leading the Way to Victory; A History of the 60th Troop Carrier Group 1940-1945* (New York: Knox Press, 2022), 208.
4   Vlahos, 208.
5   Vlahos, 224.

Of the nineteen gliders that took part in the operation, seventeen took off, eleven landed in Sicily, one released early, and it was unknown what happened to the other five.[6] The invasion of Sicily resulted in a grueling fight for every inch of territory as the Axis powers slowly retreated and multiple waves of gliders continued to bring in supplies. While the invasion of Italy (Operation AVALANCHE) included major paratroop drops, the glider portion of the invasion was called off due to high risk.

Almost a year later, on June 6, 1944, the second airborne operation, Operation OVERLORD, the invasion of Normandy, took place. The invasion consisted of Operations NEPTUNE and ANVIL. The airborne was slated to land within enemy territory and prevent the Germans from getting reinforcements to the beach and clearing the four causeways from the beach to make their way inland. Their presence caused general confusion among the German troops. They also disrupted German communications and brought in additional supplies, weapons, and ammunition. In Operation NEPTUNE, 517 CG-4As were used, an estimated 44 glider pilots were killed, and 20 were wounded.[7] The original plans, which included the invasion of Southern France (ANVIL), were canceled due to a shortage of landing craft. The operation was postponed until August 1944, when the same crafts used in the Normandy invasion could be used again. Because of a security breach, ANVIL was later renamed DRAGOON. The glider forces used in Southern France consisted of 407 CG-4As. The casualty rate was twenty-three glider pilots killed and sixty-three wounded.[8] Those casualties were not directly from the enemy but from landing zones littered with anti-glider measures and other obstacles. The objective of the airborne troops in Operations OVERLORD and ANVIL was to act as diversionary forces behind the German fortifications, secure roads, junctions,

---

6   Vlahos, 243.
7   Spencer, Leon Major USAF (ret.). "Missions," National World War II Glider Pilot Association, accessed January 17, 2023, https://www.ww2gp.og/war/missions/.
8   Spencer, "Missions."

and bridges, cut power and communication lines, and disrupt the Germans' transportation.

The next large-scale operation was scheduled for September 17, 1944. The invasion of Holland, code-named MARKET-GARDEN, called for another joint British/American airborne endeavor. The airborne conducted the MARKET segment of the operation. The focus was on taking the bridges over the Rhine. The 82nd Airborne was assigned to capture a number of bridges, including Grave and Nijmegen, and the 101st center of operations was around Eindhoven while the British were to take the northernmost bridge at Arnhem. They were also tasked with keeping the transportation corridors free from German incursion, keeping them open to allow the flow of armored vehicles and supplies and clearing the landing zones of the enemy for glider landings. The mission-support flights, delivering more troops and supplies, were to take place over several days but were badly impeded or cancelled due to weather. The weather was just one of the many factors that went into the brutal fight and failure to accomplish all the objectives of MARKET-GARDEN.

The bridge at Arnhem was, in the end, not taken by the British. The capture of the bridge at Nijmegen was delayed because General Gavin needed to secure the wooded area, Grosbeak Heights, that overlooked Nijmegen to prevent a German breakout from that area, and he was very short of men due to the non-arrival of the planned replacements due to weather. The British 30th Corps, with their tanks, were to complete the drive, opening the roadway from Valkenswaard, through Eindhoven, Veghel, Nijmegen, to Arnhem. They were unsuccessful in reaching Arnhem and, through a series of delays, were days behind schedule in reaching any of their objectives. Bad weather caused the scheduled reinforcement glider flights and drops to be cancelled or off course, and the British and Polish Airborne Brigades were cut off by the Germans and almost totally annihilated. The American airborne flew the southern portion in

1,821 CG-4As.[9] An estimated forty glider pilots were killed, thirty-seven wounded, and sixty-five reported missing in action.[10] The fighting in the southern portions eventually, and after great difficulty, opened the corridor for Allied forces to flow through. Great hopes had been placed on Market-Garden to end the war in 1944.

Not all the glider missions were preplanned. On December 26 and 27, 1944, a small contingent of glider pilots transported supplies to the 101st Airborne in Bastogne. The troops were low on ammunition, gasoline, and supplies. Their field hospital was overrun by the enemy, and they were in desperate need of medical personnel and supplies. Patton's Third Army was attempting to relieve them, but it was uncertain whether he would reach them in time. Glider pilots volunteered to transport the supplies and medical personnel to them. Sixty-one gliders were dispatched. Four glider pilots were killed, and eighteen were wounded. The encirclement resulted from Hitler's second successful attack through the treacherous terrain in the Ardennes. It was an attempt to reach the port of Antwerp, thereby forcing the Allies to create long, seemingly impossible supply lines. The Allied powers had left the Ardennes region very lightly guarded. The German Army pushed their way through, creating a "bulge" in the front lines, hence the name, "Battle of the Bulge." The Wehrmacht employed a pincer movement that had effectively encircled Bastogne before its advance was halted.[11] This was the last of Hitler's great offensives.

Shortly thereafter, on March 22, 1945, a few days before the last airborne invasion in Europe, two gliders were used in an evacuation of the seriously wounded in the battle for the Ludendorff bridge in Remagen, near Bonn, Germany. The discovery of the bridge intact

---

9   G. Thuring, *Waco CG-4A gliders in Market - Holland Sept. '44: USAAF Glider Plots - IX Troop Carrier Command* (Groesbeek, Rijk Van Nijmegen, Bevrijdings Museum 1989), 24.
10   "Missions," National World War II Glider Pilot Association, accessed January 23, 2023, https://www.ww2gp.org/war/missions/.
11   The *Wehrmacht* was the term for the Nazi military forces that included the Army, Navy and Air Force (*Luftwaffe*).

was acted upon immediately by the Allies, and a terrible battle ensued. A large part of the German resolve had melted by this time, and many of the Germans had abandoned their larger weapons, broken rank, and were evacuating across the bridge, one of the few bridges left standing across the Rhine. A victim of confusion, with troops suffering scarce supplies and a rapidly deteriorating chain of organization, the German commander Major Scheller had placed explosives on the bridge to use if necessary. They proved to be inadequate. When the explosives were detonated—literally in the face of the Allies—the bridge sustained only minor damage, which the First Army repaired while under fire. On the German side of the bridge was a long tunnel from which the Germans waged war until Major Scheller left on a bicycle in search of reinforcements. He was later shot for desertion. The bridge soon collapsed, but not before substantial numbers of US troops and supplies had crossed. Two CG-4As brought in medical supplies in the form of four thousand pounds of blankets and litters for the wounded and then evacuated the twenty-six wounded.[12] Glider evacuations were not done again in the ETO but were in the CBI. Still to come was the largest and perhaps the best enacted airborne invasion of the war—Operation VARSITY.

Operation VARSITY took place on March 24, 1945. It was part of the invasion of Central Europe and the crossing of the Rhine into Germany and tasked with the objective of capturing territory and holding it until the main body arrived; this included capturing bridges intact, enabling the Allied forces to continue to advance into Germany. It was the deadliest mission for the glider pilots in terms of casualties and probably one of the least known. It was also the last glider mission in the ETO. Towplanes hauled 906 CG-4As to landing fields around Wesel, Germany.[13] Tragically, the Germans

---

12 Hans den Brok, "Remagen," National World War II Glider Pilot Association, accessed December 15, 2023, https://www.ww2gp.og/war/missions/.
13 "Missions," National World War II Glider Pilot Association.

knew the gliders were coming in and where some of the landing zones were located. The airborne troops and glider pilots also knew that the Germans would be waiting for them. German troops had set up their weapons around the LZs and waited until the defenseless gliders were in plain view and gliding in at low altitudes of about 500 feet to land before they opened fire.[14] Some landing zones were hit harder than others—yet, to their credit, the glider pilots exhibited great skill in landing the gliders on the hot LZs and either unloaded the gliders under fire or took cover and helped take control of the landing zone and then unloaded the gliders. In Operation VARSITY, 88 glider pilots were killed, 240 wounded, and 31 were MIA.[15] The Allied victory was followed by Germany's surrender on May 7, 1945.

Gliders also were used in the China Burma India Theater of war in Operation THURSDAY, on March 5, 1944. The terrain in this theater was a huge challenge, as were the Japanese to the British. The Americans agreed to provide air support to the British Commandos. General Arnold had approved a nontraditional approach via Project 9. To defeat the Japanese in his area, British troops operating guerilla warfare in the jungle required all support by air: resupply, evacuation of wounded, and air cover. Project 9 became known as the 1st Air Commandos. Prior to Operation THURSDAY, smaller resupply missions had been conducted by the gliders in the 1st Air Commandos.[16] Their largest mission was Operation THURSDAY. Three strategic sites were chosen in the jungle to land the gliders in successive waves. The first wave was to bring the equipment, such as bulldozers, to build runways for the larger cargo/transport planes

---

14   Mark C. Vlahos, COL. USAF (ret.)" Operation Varsity," (Keynote Address, National World War II Combat Glider Pilot Association Reunion, Lubbock, Texas, October 20, 2022).
15   "Missions," National World War II Glider Pilot Association.
16   R.D. Van Wagner, *Any Place, Any Time, Any Where: The First Commandos in WWII* (Atglen PA: Schiffer 1988), 39.

to land.¹⁷ The second wave was to deliver engineers to oversee and construct the landing strips and additional troops with mules for transport. Mules were ideal modes of packing and transport in the jungle terrain; however, they were unpredictable in flight. A moving mule equaled a shifting load and one that could wreak havoc on the fragile glider. Surprisingly, by all accounts, the mules adapted to glider flight in their bamboo stalls quite well. Once the equipment and supplies were flown in in by glider, the landing strips were constructed and the C-47s, with their large transport capabilities, would take over.

The three sites chosen were Broadway and Piccadilly (March 5) and Chowringhee (March 6-7). Two of the three sites were abandoned at the last minute. The Piccadilly landing zone was strewn with logs, which would have been deadly to the gliders, personnel, and cargo they carried. Using Chowringhee without Piccadilly would effectively split the troops. This left only Broadway to dedicate the entire mission to.¹⁸ A total of sixty-four CG-4As were used; thirty-eight made it to the LZs, three were intact, and nine returned to the base at Lalaghat. Three gliders crashed shortly after takeoff; fourteen were lost en route. Eight glider pilots, copilots, and other members of the unit were killed, nineteen wounded, and twenty-one were originally missing, of which ten had been accounted for shortly thereafter.¹⁹ Many of the crashes on the landing strips were caused by debris and ruts. Additional problems consisted of snapping towropes weakening due to weather exposure and the extra strain placed on them by the double tows of overloaded gliders at high altitudes. As the towplanes began to descend from the high altitudes, the gliders,

---

17   Gary A. Best, *Silent Invaders: Combat Gliders of the Second World War*, (Fonthill Media Limited: England 2014), 19. The Airborne Tractor or bulldozer was the Clarkair Crawler Model CA-1 tractor, which was usually towed in two parts with the body of the bulldozer in one glider and the blade in another due to the full weight of the Clarkair, 4,640 pounds, heavier than the carrying capacity of the CG-4A.
18   Van Wagner, *Any Place, Any Time, Any Where*, 47.
19   1st Commando A.F., "Medical History of 1st Air Commandos," BO680 GP Cmdo-1-HI, 12/44, 72.

overloaded, began to surge forward due to weight and threatened to overtake the towplanes. They would then fall back, and the nylon towropes would stretch to their full capacity, eventually snapping.[20]

The first gliders to land on Broadway discovered only a portion of the LZ was suitable for landing, but it was too late to stop the subsequent landings that were coming in. Broadway was a costly mission, but the landing strip was built. A glider night mission consisting of twelve Hadrian gliders (the British version of the CG-4A) was set for the evening of March 6-7 into Chowringhee, and an additional landing strip was to be built.[21] The glider hauling the only bulldozer overshot the runway, and another glider loaded with a replacement bulldozer was sent in. The landing strip was successfully built. It was then abandoned due to General Wingate's concerns of the Japanese presence in the vicinity. The Japanese bombed it shortly thereafter.

The gliders continued to be used in the CBI for evacuation of the wounded using a method devised for the glider to be snatched off the ground by a C-47. One additional, smaller glider mission was conducted in Luzon, Philippine Islands, in support of the Battle of Luzon on January 25, 1945. It was very small mission consisting of six CG-4As and one CG-13A, a glider with a higher towing speed and a larger cargo capacity of eight thousand pounds.[22] It was a success with no casualties.[23] It was also the last combat glider mission flown.

---

20   Van Wagner, *Any Place, Any Time, Any Where*, 50.
21   "Chindits Special Forces Burma: Operation Thursday the 2nd Chindit Expedition" 1944, accessed January 3, 2023, https://www.chindits.info/Thursday/Operation Thursday.htm.
22   James E. Mrazek, *Fighting Gliders of World War II* (New York: St Martin's Press, 1977), 124.
23   "Missions," National World War II Glider Pilot Association.

CHAPTER 2
SILENT FLIGHT

"Please inform me what action has been taken on providing a C-47 and CG-4A for Fifth Army to get a good look at while flying over their area. Suggest you prepare an air medal and a purple heart for the crew with courage enough to do it."

—Lt. Col. J. W. Oberdorf, Memorandum to General Dunn[1]

The experimentation with airborne units, which began as early as the 1930s, resulted in the Soviets' development of a glider capable of being towed 1,170 miles.[2] By 1937, the Germans working with the Soviets developed airborne units of their own, producing the DFS-230 glider towed by commercial aircraft.[3] The German glider was of limited capacity, originally used for meteorological purposes. It was capable of transporting eight troops and a limited payload of six hundred pounds behind enemy lines.[4]

The German's successful use of the glider was the key to the opening of Western Europe to Hitler, the first objective being the successful capture of the bridges over the Albert Canal west of Maastricht intact.[5] The bridges were approximately ten kilometers

---

1 Memorandum: Lt. Col. J.W. Oberdorf to General Dun N.A.T.C.C., "Bigot" Avalanche," TC Tactics, Air Adjutant Generals WWII Combat Operations Report. 1941- 46, RG 18 Entry #7, August 15, 1943.
2 John A. McQuillen, Jr., "American Military Gliders in World War II in Europe," (Ph.D. diss., St. Louis University, 1975), 25.
3 McQuillen, 38.
4 Alan Wood, 1990, *History of the Worlds' Glider Forces* (Northamptonshire, England: Patrick Stevens Limited, 1990), 31.
5 Wood, 31.

from Fort Eben Emael. Arriving silently and capturing the bridges intact was paramount to Hitler's expansion plan to defeat France, setting the stage for attacking Britain. The glider mission to capture the bridges was conducted in conjunction with a glider mission to capture the sprawling, state-of-the-art underground Fortress Eben Emael. The Fortress was originally built in WWI and expanded upon in WWII to prevent Germany from attacking the Dutch side of the border. It also prevented the area from serving as the buffer zone for French and German hostilities toward one another. The German two-pronged attack was designed to surprise and overwhelm the forces guarding the bridge and the fort so there could be little to no effective defense mounted to delay the troops from moving rapidly toward France.

German control of the bridges would allow for large transports, equipment, and troops to cross. If they failed and the bridges, which were wired with explosives as a defensive measure, were destroyed, the German offensive would be halted and unnecessarily delayed until the area could be captured and the river crossed. All element of surprise would be lost, and the equivalent of a siege would ensue. Hitler's advantage was surprise and speed. The use of gliders allowed the engineer demolition infantry to land silently at the bridgehead on the far side of the bridge and wrest control from the forces of the defenders before they could be blown. The operation was a success, with the use of approximately thirty gliders. Germany's war machine, with all its vehicles, tanks, and equipment, could now flow across the bridges, the first barrier in Germany's path was neutralized, and the next stage could ensue unimpeded.

As planned, simultaneous to the attack on the bridges, gliders carrying a new explosive, the hollow charge silently approached and landed on the turf roof of the fortress. A total of nine of the originally slated eleven gliders landed, carrying a total of twenty-seven men. The troops dispersed according to the plan and captured the most premier fort of the day in about forty-five minutes, with a total surrender completed within a few days. On May 10, 1940, the use of the glider and airborne troops removed the second and last impediment to the gateway to France and placed the island of Britain directly within the sights of Hitler and all the forces at his command. Shortly thereafter, Hitler used his airborne troops in the Mediterranean in the very costly invasion and last major use of gliders by Germany, the invasion of Crete. Following Crete, Hitler dissolved the glider program in part because its greatest advantage, the element of complete surprise, had been lost.

Churchill responded to the German use of the airborne around 1940 and pushed the military to develop a program and train 5,000 parachute troops. The British military did so reluctantly and with consistent prodding. The British development and use of the Horsa and Hamilcar gliders allowed for large quantities of men and loads to be carried to the landing zones.[6] Their glider pilots served a dual purpose and were also trained as a very formidable infantry force. The United States continued to delay glider experimentation and production and, as late as 1936, had stated the use of long-range gliders was not a practicable weapon of "sufficient military value" to pursue.[7] America's concern was with waging a defensive rather than an offensive war, in which the glider would have no place.[8] It was in 1941 that the Army Air Corps began to seriously look at studying the use of the combat glider.[9]

The delay was reflected in the United States Army Air Forces' Glider Pilot Programs' primary emphasis on flight instruction, pushing

---

6 Mrazek, *Fighting Gliders of World War II*, 62. The British used three gliders, the American CG-4A, which they called the "Hadrian"; the Horsa, which was larger the CG-4A, made of wood; and the Hamilcar, which was the "largest wooden aircraft built during WWII" and had a 110-foot wingspan. Both the Horsa and the Hamilcar could carry large weapons and vehicles. Some American glider pilots liked flying the Horsa, but many did not, one reason being the larger size and larger weight both loaded and unloaded made it difficult, if not impossible, to land and stop in smaller landing zones.
7 McQuillen, *American Military Gliders in WWII in Europe*, 27.
8 Danielle R. Mortensen, Historian, Tactical Aviation, Office of Air Force History, interview by author, Bolling Air Force Base, Washington, D.C., 19 April 1989.
9 Mrazek, *Fighting Gliders of World War II*, 99.

the need for infantry combat training aside until 1943.[10] Prior to the installation of a serious combat training program, the individual glider pilots' performance in the ETO was severely impaired. America's attempt to define and develop the glider program while embarking in war led to political infighting, jostling for position, vague objectives, inadequate supplies, virtual isolation, and inconsistent infantry training in both frequency and subject matter. All these imposed handicaps were overcome only by the glider pilots' sagacity, single-mindedness, and determination in combat.

THE GLIDER

When considered as a military transport to be used in combat, the CG-4A glider used in World War II had an unusual structure and design. Initially, its greatest asset was the element of surprise it afforded and Hitler so valued. Later, it was recognized more for its ability to land in relatively small fields behind enemy lines and deliver men and weapons in close proximity to each other. The glider infantry constituted an effective fighting force ready for immediate action as soon as the glider was unloaded. The gliders cargo-carrying capabilities were paramount and need to be highlighted. A glimpse into a few of the operations demonstrates the weight the glider pilots and their CG-4As threw behind the Allied forces.

According to the 1944 IX Troop Carrier Statistical Control Office, *Consolidated Tactical Operational Summary*, the following amounts of cargo and men were delivered to the battlefields in the ETO: Operation NEPTUNE (Normandy), June 6-7: 512 gliders, 4,047 troops delivered to their objective, 43 not landed on their objective, 110 artillery weapons landed, 281 jeeps, and 412,477 pounds of combat equipment and supplies landed.[11] Operation

---

10   Maurer Maurer, ed., *Air Force Combat Units of World War II*, (Washington D.C.: Office of Air Force History, 1983), 8-9.
11   Headquarters IX Troop Carrier Command, Statistical Control Office, *Consolidated Tactical Operational Summary Operations "Neptune - "Dragoon"- "Market."*

DRAGOON (Southern France), August 15-16: 316 gliders, 2,235 troops delivered to their objective, 26 not landed on their objective, 59 artillery weapons landed, 175 jeeps, and 409,709 pounds of combat equipment and supplies landed.[12] Operation MARKET (Holland), September 17-30: 1,899 gliders, 9,566 troops landed on objective, 1,432 troops not landed on their objective, 185 artillery weapons landed, 705 jeeps, and 2,476,594 pounds of combat equipment and supplies landed.[13] The *totals* combined on these three operations, which spanned a four month period of 1944, were as follows: 2,727 gliders dispatched, 15,848 troops landed on the objective, 1,501 troop not landed on the objective, 354 artillery landed, 1,161 jeeps, and 3,298,730 pounds of combat equipment and supplies delivered.[14]

Gliders were heavily relied upon, albeit in lesser numbers, in the China Burma India Theater. Figures that are available estimate the glider portion of *Operation THURSDAY* delivered 221,648 pounds listed on their manifests.[15] It is important to highlight and keep in mind that even though the gliders were used in combat as early as 1943, their tactical abilities were not fully defined or taught to students until 1944.

During the initial stages of The Glider Pilot Program, numerous glider designs were tested by the United States AAC. The Waco CG-4A model was not the only one accepted and put into production, but it was the one most frequently used in combat. Design and testing aside, manufacturing the gliders proved to be another problem. Because it was wartime, the current output of planes could not be sacrificed; therefore, no power plane manufacturers were to be used in glider production. Eventually, manufacturing contracts

---

12   Statistical Control Office, *Consolidated Tactical Operational Summary Operations "Neptune - "Dragoon"- "Market."*
13   Statistical Control Office, *Consolidated Tactical Operational Summary Operations "Neptune - "Dragoon"- "Market.";* G. Thuring quotes 2,520 gliders in American and British Gliders, 24.
14   Statistical Control Office, *Consolidated Tactical Operational Summary Operations "Neptune - "Dragoon"- "Market."*
15   Van Wagner, *Any Place, Any Time, Any Where*, 54.

were signed with sixteen companies.[16] In order to meet production deadlines, they, in turn, subcontracted parts to companies such as Steinway and Sons Piano Manufacturers, H.J. Heinz Pickle Co., Anheuser-Busch, and Gardner Metal Products.[17] Inevitable production problems plagued the program throughout the war, causing a domino effect and resulting in major training delays for the pilots. The glider was made up of 70,000 parts, and production of the parts was subcontracted. Some of the companies subcontracted to produce parts, and those contracted to produce the glider had poor management and quality control. This resulted in costs running over and failed deliveries.[18]

Poor quality control also resulted in many tragic accidents, one of which is the well documented glider crash in St. Louis, Missouri, with the St. Louis mayor and other dignitaries on board in 1943. The takeoff in front of a field of viewers was excellent, but shortly after the towrope was released, the right wing broke off. The glider plunged nose down into the ground, killing all aboard. The continuation of the glider program was in serious threat of cancellation after this tragic display. After investigations were conducted, it was determined that the fitting that held the wing strut to the fuselage caused the wing structural failure. During production at the Gardner Metal Products Company, it had been bored too deeply.[19] This caused a structural weakness, and the metal fitting snapped, releasing the wing. The manufacturer of the glider, Robertson Aircraft, never examined the part when it was

---

16   Mrazek, *Fighting Gliders of World War II*, 202.The companies were Ford, WACO, Gibson, Commonwealth, Northwestern, G&A, General, Ridgefield, Robertson, Pratt-Read, Laister-Kauffman, Cessna, Babcock, Timm, Ward, and National.
17   Gerard M. Devlin, *Silent Wings: The Saga of the U.S. Army and Marine Combat Glider During World War II*, 1st U.S. Ed. (New York: St. Martin's press, 1985), 302. Parts manufactured by these companies include wings, tail surfaces, and struts.
18   Flint Whitlock, "Getting the Glider off the Ground," Warfare History Network, excerpt from Flint Whitlock, If Chaos Reigns) The Near Disasters and Ultimate Triumph of Allied Airborne Forces on D-Day June 6, 1944, (Casemate, 1944), https://warfarehistorynetwork.com/getting-the-gliders-off-the-ground/.
19   Whitlock, "Getting the Glider off the Ground."

received from Gardner.[20] Even more concerning is that 25 percent of these same parts in the inventory at Robertson were manufactured in the same way.[21] The Army Inspector General's office concluded that this same situation was probably prevalent throughout the country. In March of 1944, additional gliders were grounded "pending an investigation of improper quality control and the use of unauthorized materials at Robertson and a subcontractor, Anheuser-Busch."[22]

The CG-4A's basic construction utilized light materials designed to reduce the strain on the tow craft. The fuselage, which measured forty-eight feet long, was forged of lightweight steel tubing, as was the frame of the entire glider. The wings were constructed of plywood sheets attached to a wooden frame and had a total wingspan of 83.6 feet.[23] The floor was constructed in a honeycombed plywood reinforced on the sides to carry heavy equipment.[24] The entire skeleton was then covered with a cotton/linen fabric, painted with layers of a chemical compound, and finally painted camouflage green.[25]

The finished product had a payload of 3,750 pounds and a glide ratio of 12 to 1 when fully loaded (12 feet of glide per 1 foot of descent), and 15 to 1 when empty.[26] The rate of descent in a loaded

---

20 Whitlock, "Getting the Glider off the Ground."
21 Whitlock, "Getting the Glider off the Ground."
22 Whitlock, "Getting the Glider off the Ground."
23 Mrzaek, *Fighting Gliders*, 111.
24 Mrzaek, 107.
25 Sharon McCullar, curator of the Silent Wings Museum, described the materials and processes of applying and sealing the fabric on the glider. The fabric was a woven cotton fabric with a weight similar to muslin or a tightly woven broadcloth. It was stretched over the frame and then shrunk to fit the frame by the use of steam. It was then coated with up to thirteen layers of "Dope." Dope was alternated with layers of formulations soluble in Butyrate and Acetate, which would adhere to the fabric and previous layers of dope. This would continue to tighten the fabric around the frame. The chemical coatings being synthetic, they melted when the glider burned, and the cotton fabric underneath ignited into flames. Dope was a type of varnish or lacquer, which created the smoother surface and can improve the aerodynamic performance of the glider. National World War II Glider Pilots Association.
26 Lt. Col. Paul W. Mousseau (USAF Ret.), WWII glider pilot of the 314th TCG, 32nd TCS, and a veteran of Sicily, Normandy, Southern France, Holland, and Varsity, interview by author, 20 June 1989, Fresno California.

glider was approximately 400 feet per minute, with a landing run of 600 to 800 feet.[27] The glide ratio was impacted by a number of factors, one being the wind conditions the glider was flying in. Weight was also a factor. An overloaded glider increased weight of the glider and shortened the glide ratio. Heavier gliders usually required a longer distance to stop after landing. To keep the weight down and increase the glide ratio, armor plating was sacrificed, and the glider occupants were predisposed to injury or death from enemy antiaircraft guns and small-arms fire.

The CG-4A glider flown in WWII had a fuselage that measured 48 feet long and a total wingspan of 83.6 feet. The glider went through changes as the war progressed. Toward the latter part of the war, a metal nose protection called the "Griswold nose" was installed on some gliders and saved lives. The wheels could be ejected, and in this photograph, the skids are visible on the very front undercarriage. Some

---

27 Office of Flying Safety, Headquarters AAF, "Pilot Training Manual for the CG-4A Glider," March 1945. Reprinted by George E. Peterson, n.d., 14.

glider pilots reported that the skids gave them less control because they dug in and continued moving the gliders on one trajectory despite attempts to steer in another direction. Photo courtesy of the Silent Wings Museum Foundation of the Military Glider Pilots Association.

The photo shows the interior of a CG-4A 15-place combat glider used during World War II by the American IX Troop Carrier Command. In this model, one steering column was swung back and forth between the pilot and copilot. In other models, there are two steering columns. The wooden benches pictured on the sides were for the glider infantry to sit. They were removeable so larger cargo could be lashed down inside. Although not clearly visible, the entire front and sides of the cockpit was plexiglass, affording the pilots clear views. The section where the pilots sat would swing upward to load and unload the cargo. It had an unintended benefit that, when unlatched by the pilots, it could move them out of the way of forward shifting loads on landing or impact and prevent serious injuries. Note the lack of any armament to protect the occupants from enemy fire or obstacles penetrating the *exterior. Photo courtesy of the Silent Wings Museum Foundation of the Military Glider Pilots Association.*

The absence of a hard, protective covering rendered the gliders unable to withstand obstacles encountered in the assigned landing zones.[28] Injuries to the pilots and troops were caused by tree branches, posts, bullets, and other items when they pierced the glider's exterior. Lt. William A. Bryant of the 95th TCS reported on his return from his mission, March 26, 1945,

> Fabric and windshield taken away & shell holes.... On landing, a fence post of diameter 8" x 8" came through nose and hit me on the inside of right knee, cutting and badly spraining it. This hampered my activity for the entire operation.[29]

Lt. Cobb, the gliders copilot, and Second Lt. Appleman, the pilot, encountered anti-glider poles on the landing zone in Normandy. The report was filed by Lt. Cobb:

> Did not receive any flak till we got close in. Landed at (30.8) - (89.1). There were posts (50' apart) and 10' to 12' high in the fields. They were wood and 8" in diameter. This field was 5 miles S.W. of LZ in enemy territory. Clipped off tip right wing when we hit obstacles (2 poles cut off.) I made a good landing Load: 57mm howitzer and 3 A/B ems [enlisted men]![30]

---

28 Later in the war, a conical-shaped metal covering was applied to the nose of the glider to protect the occupants. It was called a "Griswold nose"; however, they were only installed on some gliders.
29 Lt. William A. Bryant, 440th TCG 95th TCS, "Troop Carrier Mission Glider Interrogation Check Sheet" (hereafter referred to as "TCMICS-GP"), RG 18 Entry #7, Federal Records Center, Suitland, Md.
30 Lt. Walter L. Cobb and 2nd Lt. Stratton M. Appleman, Handwritten Account, RG 18 Entry#7, 437th TCG, Federal Records Center, Suitland, Md.

METHOD OF OPERATION

Large transport planes, usually C-47s, towed gliders into battle either singularly or in pairs. During a single tow, the glider was attached to the towplane by a 350-foot nylon rope, 11/16 inches in diameter, with metal fittings, although the towropes differed with the different models of gliders.[31] On double tows, one glider was towed on a 350-foot towrope; the second glider rope had 75 feet added to it, making it 425 feet long.[32]

Pictured is American glider pilots behind a C-47 towplanes in a double tow formation. On the far right, two gliders on different length towropes can be seen being hauled by the towplane on the lower center. Pictured front and center is another CG-4A, and the tow tope attachment point can be seen. Photo courtesy of the Silent Wings Museum Foundation of the Military Glider Pilots Association.

---

31   Charles Day, Historian, NWWIIGPA, email message to author, Association April 2023.
32   Charles Day email.

There were both speed and load limitations. According to the 1945 Pilot Training Manual for the CG-4A, the maximum designed speed on tow or in free flight was 150 mph. The permissible maximum speeds fell lower as the load limitations went up. For 7,500 pounds gross weight (LGW), the maximum permitted Calibrated Air Speed (CAS) was 150 mph, and the maximum permissible Indicated Air Speed (IAS) was 158 mph. At 8,000 LGW, the maximum permissible CAS was 143, and the maximum permissible IAS was 151 mph. If the gross weight moved up to 8,500 pounds, the maximum permissible CAS was 135 mph, and the maximum permissible IAS was 143 mph, and when the maximum emergency gross weight of 9,000 pounds was reached, the gliders maximum permissible CAS was 128 mph, and the maximum permissible IAS was 136 mph.[33] This final weight was not to be exceeded.

The stall speed of the glider was based on a 7,500-pound load and was 49 to 60 mph, the tactical glide speed (landing speed) was 60 to 70 mph, and the normal glide speed was 72.6 to 85 mph.[34] Both of these glide speeds were with a designed load. The glider pilot positioned the glider to avoid as much turbulence from the tow craft as possible and concentrated on preventing the glider from moving too far in any one direction and keeping the correct tension on the towrope.[35] This was very difficult, if not impossible, to discern when flying through heavy overcast or cloudy conditions. The glider pilots relied on the angle of the towrope portion that they could see when visibility or weather conditions were too bad to have a visual of their towplane.

---

33   Office of Flying Safety, Headquarters AAF, "Pilot Training Manual for the CG-4A Glider," 14.
34   Office of Flying Safety, Headquarters AAF, "Pilot Training Manual for the CG-4A Glider," 14.
35   Bigot Dragoon "Instructions to Glider Pilots," RG 18 Entry #7, Box 1191, Federal Records Center, Suitland, MD. In the Invasion of Southern France, bulldozers with the blade attached were hauled in by glider. The gliders were placed at the head of the formation to avoid all possible turbulence and would be the first to release for safety reasons since they would have the maximum amount of sink. The gliders were well over the maximum load specified but did not exceed 9,000 lbs.

The tow pilots could communicate with the glider through a series of lights indicating "release." There was an intercom system between the two aircrafts, but it did not always work. At Sedalia Army Airfield, instructions were given to the glider pilots for emergency signals from their towplanes. The lights were emitted from the astral dome on the tow ship; however, the lights were not visible during the daytime. Glider training and operation procedures state the towplane pilots alerted the glider pilots to their arrival over the LZ in two minutes by flashing a red "alert" light, followed by a flashing green "go" light at one minute out. [36] Other sources report a different version of lights; a red light meant the glider will release the towrope in thirty seconds, while a blinking red light indicated the glider was to cut immediately.[37] When the intercom was not working, the towplane and glider communicated through the movement of their respective aircrafts, which could be seen or felt by the other.

At the point of release in normal operations the glider pilots hit their towrope release mechanisms and headed in for landing, sometimes by the hundreds. The release mechanism in the towplane was supposed to be used only in the case of an emergency or to drop the rope away from the LZ before flying the return leg of the trip. Regardless, there were times when a glider was released by its tow ship prematurely for any number of reasons, forcing the glider pilot to bring his ship down as best he could while evaluating landing conditions such as speed, approach, winds, weather, visibility, terrain, obstacles, other gliders, men on the field, and time of day or night. With the absence of power to resume altitude, his knowledge of soaring, sheer ingenuity, and survival instinct had to be combined to bring the glider down safely. Because this type of situation was always a possibility, the glider pilots remained on constant alert for

---

36 "Glider Training and Operational Procedures," September 1944, Reel BO543, 58. Air Force Historical Research Agency, Maxwell AFB.
37 "Maneuver," 61st Troop Carrier Wing, Sedalia Army Airfield, Warrensburg, Mo., October 20, 1944. 2, RG 18 Entry #7 Federal Records Center, Suitland, Md.

a suitable landing field, anywhere, anytime.[38] Flight Officer Larkin found himself released over German-held territory when he was given the green light by his tow pilot.

> This was a double tow assault and Johnny Boersig was on with me . . . a few minutes over the Rhine River Capt. Deere who was leading our 4 towplane (8 gliders) element took a direct hit, caught on fire and came out of control directly across in front of our entire flight. We were echelon to the right and Deere was headed straight for [name omitted] tow ship. [Name omitted] pulled up and turned sharp right out of formation and Boersig and I followed - we were then out alone over German held territory taking some hell roaring ground fire. [Name omitted] showed a green light in his astro dome bubble and so Boersig and I had to cut loose and land . . . [Name omitted] high tailed in back across the Rhine . . . BASTARD . . . Boersig and I landed in the same field and caught rifle and mortar fire for awhile. Wesel was only half a mile away and after a few hours some British commandos who had occupied wesel during the night came out and rescued us from our exposed positions . . . only one-man out of our two gliders had been shot by the Germans, there were about 10 of us altogether.[39]

---

38 Although the tow pilots had the ability to release the gliders, it was stressed that they were to do so only in an emergency. If the glider was cut off, the tow ship was to circle it, drop a raft if over water, and immediately report its location. There were instances, however, when this procedure was not followed. The greatest danger, in any case of the tow ship releasing first, was the tendency of the towrope and hook to hurl back through the gliders' windshield or wrap itself around a wing or the tail, shearing it off. Other tow pilots were more conscientious, locating lost gliders and reporting their whereabouts if the original tow had failed to do so. Relations could be tenuous between glider pilots and tow pilots. Toward the end of the war, when relations had greatly improved to some extent, numerous tow pilots lost their lives flying into virtual suicidal situations to ensure the safe release of the gliders and men they were towing.

39 Flight Officer Larkin handwritten notes on war memorabilia shared by his son, Michael Larkin, NWWIIGPA researcher, email with author May 23, 2023.

This CG-4A suffered wing damage in Southern France, Operation Dragoon. F/O Collin R. Beeson originally attached to the 442nd TCG 93rd TCS wrote a description in 1984. "I carried 14 glider troopers with all their equipment. We landed in a grape arbor that had quite a few anti-glider poles that we manage to weave through. You can see that the wings were damaged, but no one was hurt. Also, the undercarriage was ripped out due to the vines." Photo courtesy of Silent Wings Museum.

Whatever conditions prevailed, the glider pilots planned their approach and brought the gliders in at various speeds, which ranged from a near stalling speed of fifty miles per hour to low approach quick landings at upwards of one hundred miles per hour. Other times, they were approaching at excessive speeds and had to use obstacles and flying maneuvers to slow the glider. The amount of damage to the glider, pilots, copilot, passengers, and equipment depended on the obstacles and gliders on and around the landing fields, the number of gliders trying to land on the same LZ, and the amount of enemy fire hitting the glider on its approach and landing. In Operation Varsity, Second Lieutenant Crowell was a power pilot acting as a copilot (power glider pilot) to Flight Officer Reed. Lieutenant Crowell's observations are a testament to the constant alertness and skill the glider pilots exhibited under stress.

> I do not think we were hit much, if any by flak but we did take s/a [small arms] hits aft. The airborne were remarkably cool during it all and earned my sincere admiration. At first we had difficulty locating our field in the haze. F/O Reed, my pilot, spotted it finally and made a beautiful landing by passing over a fence, under some telephone wires and between the telephone poles and the trees on our left. We hit smoothly and stopped quite fast.[40]

Flight Officer Warren DeBeauclair also flew in the same operation. He reported the landing zone was filled with high tension wires, telephone poles, fences, and trees. On their approach, they were hit with intense machine gun, small arms fire, and mortars.

> Went in 270° over high-tension wires and over two fences and had a good slow landing. Landed at 202 - 461 20 yards from the burnt house where automatic weapons opened fire on us. Hit the dirt next to the glider away from the house. 2 snipers in the wood 60 yds. away opened fire on us & kept us flat for 1 hr. 10 minutes. We crawled under the glider to cover the airborne who was attacking the house & just got to the other side of the glider when it was hit by mortar & the jeep still inside. The

---

40 F/O Bill Audrey Reed and 2nd Lt. Christopher C. Crowell, "TCMICS-GP," Varsity, RG 18 Entry #7, Federal Records Center, Suitland, Md.

glider went up in flames. . . . the PFC was killed and burned.[41]

Glider pilots' reports demonstrates the variety of dangers that existed on the landing zones:

> Shortly after a glider crashed into the trees directly above (25:10 - 43:00) and only by luck did we escape being hit by the glider and debris. This glider was piloted by F/O Fred Tuck and F/O Harry Zonge. F/O Tuck had been shot through the leg while in flight and F/O Zonge had been hit in the neck by flak. F/O Tuck managed to get out but F/O Zonge was caught and unconscious.[42]

> Observed one C-47 fall out of control, one glider cartwheel on landing and also another glider fall out of control while burning fiercely.[43]

In his book, *The Glider Gang*, Milton Dank recounts the approach and landing of Major Hugh Nevins and Lt. Bob Burke. As they approached the LZ, the light to moderate flak and small arms fire increased to intense, and Dank described the skill of the glider pilots as they came in at about 120 mph and 100 mph on their final turn. To slow the glide quickly, they had to do an "immediate nose-high stall and left slide slip."[44] In order to get the left wing back up, it took both the pilot and copilot "riding the controls together."[45] The maneuver slowed the gliders speed in half, from 100 mph to 50 mph. They

---

41 F/O Warren DeBeauclair, "Troop Carrier Mission Glider Interrogation Check Sheet" (hereinafter referred to as "TCMGICS,") RG 18 Entry #7, 95th TCS, Varsity, Federal Records Center, Suitland, Md.
42 Unidentified Author, 437th TCG, RG 18 Entry #7, Federal Records Center, Suitland, Md.
43 F/O James R. Bousman, 437th TCG 86th TCS, "TCMICS-GP," Varsity, RG 18 Entry #7 Federal Records Center, Suitland, Md.
44 Milton Dank, *The Glider Gang*, 249-250.
45 Dank, 249-250.

described the glider infantry as "dull airsick troops" after the flight.[46]

The airsick troops in Major Nevins's glider were known as "glider riders," the airborne infantry who had not volunteered to arrive at the battlefield in gliders but were ordered to do so. They flew in without parachutes and were seated on the plywood benches lining the fabric walls or in the vehicle being transported. They were virtually defenseless against enemy strafing while riding in the glider during flight and landing and often after landing, prior to getting out. Flight Officers Admietz and King's report following Operation Varsity in 1945 reflects the devastation enemy fire could inflict on the defenseless occupants of the glider:

> Received direct hit, 2 min. past Rhine lost control and cut. After we cut we were hit again. In nose by A.A. [anti-aircraft fire] and small arms. Load consisted of 12 A/B [airborne] and all were wounded. One A/B dead. Pilot received flak in left arm and CP [copilot] received wound in left leg. All jumped from glider upon landing and were fired upon. Removed wounded and gave them first aid. . . . We were the first glider to land in Germany.[47]

Second Lieutenant Claude Myer, again in Varsity, watched from behind as his tow pilot had his right engine shot out and it caught fire. Lt. Meyers last sight of his towplane was someone trying to get out the escape hatch of the flaming plane after its pilots risked everything to get them to the correct landing zone. Despite the tow pilot's best efforts, Myers was forced to release his towrope and would not make his LZ on the glide he had remaining. His report documents the challenges the glider occupants faced both in the air and once on the ground:

---

46 Dank, 249-250.
47 F/O George L. King and F/O Ignatius E. Adamietz Jr., "TCMICS-GP," RG 18 Entry #7, 437th TCG, G.P.s Attached and Assigned to 83rd TCS, Federal Records Center, Suitland, Md.

> We glided straight ahead and lost some altitude then did a 90 degree turn to the left and hit a telephone pole with our right wing and made a pretty hard landing. We came to a stop about halfway through a hedgerow. We all got out alright. No was hurt in the landing. My pilot and myself crawled to the front of another glider which was hit by mortar fire and my pilot was hit. He was dying and there was nothing I could do for him. By this time two airborne men were about 15 feet in front of me and they were hit by mortar fire and blown up. I didn't know what to do except to lie there which I did for about 3/4 of an hour and then some airborne came up and I went with them to the CP and dug in for the night.... All I got out of my glider was my carbine everything else was burned.[48]

Extensive damage to the glider controls from enemy fire was another possibility. Oftentimes, pilots lost their rudders, stabilizers, and ailerons—necessitating immediate, uncontrolled landings.

To add to the list of potential dangers was the heavy equipment transported in gliders, which could cause serious casualties if it shifted forward at any time during flight or landing. To avoid being crushed by vehicles that broke their lashings, the pilots took advantage of the CG-4A's hinged cockpit. Initially designed to enable jeeps, bulldozers, trailers, and howitzers to be loaded, the entire front portion of the fuselage was hinged to the body of the plane. The cockpit was held shut by a catch, controlled by the nose release lever located between the two pilots. A cable was attached to the inside nose of the CG-4A, ran across the top of the glider, and attached to the tail end of a jeep. As long as the lashings held the jeep stationary, the cockpit remained closed. If the lashings broke, the jeep was catapulted forward, sometimes at speeds up to seventy miles per hour. Its forward thrust automatically pulled the cable, which opened

---

48 2nd Lt. Claude Myers, "TCMICS-GP," 437th TCG, 84th TCS, Varsity March 27-29 '45, Serial A-8, RG 18 Entry #17, Federal Records Center, Suitland, Md.

the nose and raised the pilots to safety from shifting cargo. In the CBI, the same configuration was made for the bulldozers to avoid the glider pilots being crushed if it broke loose.

The glider pilots made good use of this feature. Lt. Col. Paul Mousseau recounted how it was common practice to release the lever as soon as possible, often on the final approach if heavy equipment was being hauled. This would prevent the pilots and troops from being injured in the event of shifting cargo or head-on collisions.[49] Once raised, the cockpit was designed to remain locked in the upright position. However, injuries caused by the forceful upward swing of the nose, which then sometimes broke off, were not uncommon. Flight Officers Wharton and Locke took advantage of the hinged cockpit upon finding their landing zone filled with obstacles:

> In the final approach to landing we saw a field in which the Germans had set up posts twenty to fifteen feet in height and about one foot in diameter, with wire strung from the top to the bottom of these posts. I pulled the nose of my glider up to prevent it from crashing into these obstacles but landed in a field constructed somewhat in the American manner. I then pulled the nose release back to prevent the jeep from crushing in the nose of the glider if it broke loose. Upon landing and hitting these posts we assumed that the jeep did break loose because the nose flew up and the jeep went out with 1st Lt. [Lt. Corn] and bicycle in it and we never saw them again. I was pinned in the nose of the Glider by my safety belt. The nose then came off. Horton was thrown clear of the glider in landing. He came back and got me out. At this time the machine gun nest began to fire on us that was about 60 yards away. we were trying to locate the jeep and Lt. Corn with the light of the flares to aid us but we could not locate the jeep or Lt. Corn. ... F/O Wharton received a bruised leg and lost three

---

49   Mousseau, interview, 20 June 1989.

teeth. ... F/O Locke received an injured back, sprained ankle and a cut over the eyes. Our glider was torn all to hell - it had both wings torn off and the nose section damaged.[50]

The CG-4A's cockpit could be lifted to enable the loading of jeeps, bulldozers, and howitzers. To do this, the tail of the plane was lifted, and the ramps built into the glider folded down. The jeep was then lashed in. Photo courtesy of the Silent Wings Museum Foundation of the Military Glider Pilots Association.

But the mechanism for the nose lift was not infallible; sometimes the nose would not lift, and, other times, it was unable to lift due to an obstruction. Lt. Ittner's glider hit an embankment at high-speed with the nose of the glider making impact. He reported the deadly force of the impact of the weight of the cargo shifting forward on the

---

50 F/O Whorton and F/O Clarence Locke, Invasion of Normandy, "Glider Pilot Interrogation" (hereafter referred to as "GPI"), RG18 Entry #7, 437th TCG. Federal Records Center, Suitland, Md.

occupants in the jeep and the inability of the glider pilots to get out of the way as they were sandwiched between the shifting cargo and the embankment the glider hit:

> No shots were fired directly at us until after making landfall, and then all hell broke loose. Looked like five guns were pyramiding a cross fire and we had to fly through it. We were hit often. We descended through the overcast and emerged about two miles from the L.Z. A couple of F.W. 190's or ME-109s strafed us ... The 2nds fire got the controls on our right aileron. It also hit the towrope and the rope was spinning and unwinding. By this time we were pretty close to the LZ and was receiving ground fire which blew off our rudder control. I saw a field, tried to turn but had no control. I got the left wing down and made a shallow bank at 180°. ... We hit the bank on the opposite side of the field and busted the nose of the glider. The jeep broke loose, rolling forward pinning Dick (copilot) and myself against the nose and the bank.
>
> My passengers, Airborne Captain Nick W. Russel and Cpl. Floyd E. Mapes, were in the jeep. The jeep bent in middle and pinned them in the seat. Schank and Stone had landed in the same field about 400 feet north of us and sent one of their Airborne passengers, a sergeant, to help us. He helped to get me out and I don't remember all the details of this particular time. He then worked on Dick and finally got him out. I snapped out of it about fifteen minutes later and we laid Dick out after finding that he had broken or fractured his ankle, he was unable to walk and pretty groggy. ... The Corporal was then released from the jeep without too much trouble but the Captain was unconscious and pinned for about an hour while we worked to get him out. He was in great pain and semi-conscious. We finally got him out by cutting a hole through the roof and sliding him down the wing which had

bent around close to the fuselage. We used the aileron for a stretcher and removed the Captain with the aid of a few paratroopers who had joined us.

Schank and I carried Levering on a gun to a hedge row and ditch for cover. Meanwhile there was fire in most all directions, although we were receiving no direct fire. We got a couple of Bazookas and hand grenades and holed up in the ditch. The Captain was given two shots of morphine without effect. Later we gave him another. He had a broken hip, crushed knee, broken leg, chest crushed and face all banged up. The Corporal walked up but later passed out. We didn't know where we were and remained in this spot for about four hours. I gave a French kid that came along two hundred (200) francs to take a note seeking aid to the Americans who were, he said, over the hill behind the German lines. But after an exchange of notes no medical aid was available. [51]

A further major cause of fatalities was explosive cargo. Then 1st Lt. Paul W. Mousseau flew the lead serial A-22 in Operation Varsity as a copilot, with Captain Morris Scott as pilot; their glider was being towed by Lt. Col. Halac G. Wilson. Lt. Mousseau had his picture taken just one hour prior to takeoff on Operation VARSITY with two other glider pilots, friends from his initial training and the 314th Troop Carrier Group; they had all survived the war this far—to the last mission in the ETO. Their names were Lt. Lorne F. Bulpitt and Lt. Duane E. Ellis, and the cargo they were hauling was highly explosive. Below is Lt. Mousseau's eyewitness account of their last flight:

Bulpitt and Ellis were carrying a load of gasoline - their glider exploded when it hit the L.Z. and it was just a ball of fire. I

---

51 Headquarters 437th TCG, "Statement of 1st Lt. Evans A. Ittner and F/O Richard G. Levering," RG 18 Entry #7, 437th TCG, Federal Records Center, Suitland, Md. Lt. Ittner's handwritten note to the medic and the responses to it can be seen on page 36.

saw one of them lying there afterwards. Ellis was about six feet tall, but I couldn't tell who it was because the body was blackened and shrunk to about four feet. I didn't see his dog tags on but even if I had I wouldn't have touched them the body was so badly burnt. Graves registration had been around and was coming back in about an hour. It made me feel bad, real bad to see them.[52]

> Need medical aid immediately – Messenger will lead you to us – No hostile activities in this immediate vicinity.
>
> Evans A. Stuer
> 1st Lt. A.C.
> O-377167
>
> No medical aid around – we have man here with bullet wound in shoulder.
> OVER

---

52   Mousseau, interview, 20 June 1989.

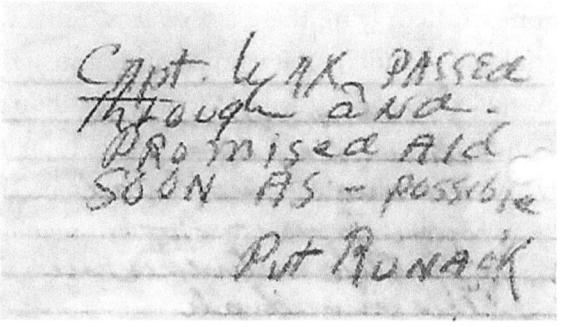

F/O Ittner's note requesting medical aide in the Invasion of Normandy. The original note was located in a box with glider pilot interrogation reports at one of the archives during the author's research.[53]

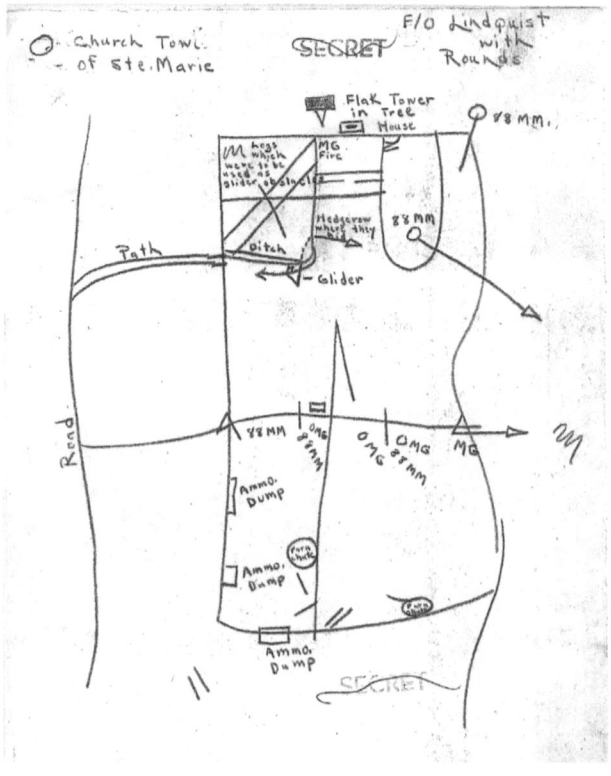

---

53   Note to Medic, Lt. Ittner, 437th TCG, RG18, Entry #7, Federal Records Center, Suitland, Md.

F/O Vincent C. Lindquist, 85th TC Sq. 437th TC Gp., co-pilot of F/O Leon V. Rounds map of landing zone and their movements. Upon landing they jumped into a ditch of chest high water under crossfire from machine guns.

The glider pilots had aptly nicknamed the gliders "flying coffins" in part because of the casualty rates and in part because the steel fittings that were used to attach the wings struts to the fuselage of the glider were manufactured by a coffin company, Gardner Metal Products Company.[54] Looking at photographs of glider crashes from the war, it seems a miracle anyone survived. Flight Officer Charles L. Brema reported following a mission.

> . . . The glider flown by Baker and Magistro was seen to fly into a clump of trees at the end of a field. According to one observer it disintegrated as it crashed. We heard nothing definite as to what had happened to the pilot and copilot, but on board the barge where we spent the night, someone, apparently a member of the crew stated that two bodies had been carried away from the wreckage of a glider which bore the identifying number of this glider. ... We viewed the wrecked glider flown by Lt. Overall and F/O Weiss. The latter's body was lying on the ground with his head badly smashed. . . . Lt. Overall was badly injured and taken to the hospital. I went over to the field where the glider flown by F/Os Schultz and R.W. Smith was lying, and it was a mass of kindling. I saw a body with the legs hanging over the seat. A civilian offered to permit him to be carried to his farmhouse a short distance away. A medical officer who was present at the crash stated that this should not be done, since F/O Smith

---

54 R. Ray Otensie, "Gliders: From Wright Field to the Netherlands," Wright Patterson AFB, September 16, 2019, https://www.wpafb.af.mil/News/Article-Display/Article/1961634/flashback-glidersfrom-wright-field-to-the-netherlands/.

would be dead within five minutes.[55]

An American fifteen-place CG-4A glider did not clear the trees at Wesel, Germany, after flying across the Rhine River in Operation Varsity. One of the issues, especially in Normandy, was briefings that cited smaller hedges, not fifty-foot trees. The gliders had very little lift after being cut loose and often could not clear obstacles if the intelligence was inaccurate. They did, however, sometimes use trees, which hit their wings to slow their landing speed. Photo courtesy of the Silent Wings Museum Foundation of the Military Glider Pilots Association.

Despite assurances from the Army Air Corps, the glider pilots believed they had become as expendable as the aircraft they flew. This is borne out by statements made in the 1945 Pilot Training Manual for the CG-4A Glider. Under "YOUR JOB" it states, "Contrary to popular belief, the glider is not limited to a single mission, neither are

---

55   F/O Charles L. Brema, "Mission Reports," RG 18 Entry #7, 93rd TCS, 8/44-2/45, Federal Records Center, Suitland, Md.

you."[56] As early as 1943, after explaining what the role and training of the glider pilot was, a report on troop carrier aviation, cautioned that " Parachute and glider troops are not to be regarded as suicide forces."[57] If the author of that statement did not intend to include glider pilots, he should have. Many glider pilots suffered substantial injuries, including major blows to the head while landing. They also engaged in fighting alone and with the airborne. They often died where they landed.

Some argue, considering the dangers involved, the death ratio for glider pilots was relatively low. Others contend the casualties were higher than reported. No official killed-in-action list for glider pilots was ever compiled by the Army Air Forces. The numbers today and those cited in this book are estimates only. Many men were buried in the fields where they landed, other counted as infantry casualties. As for the small minority of gliders that were salvageable, only a relative few in comparison to the numbers produced were ever "picked up" and reused on later missions.[58] The remainder were not salvageable due to the damage incurred during flight and landing, strips of fabric siding being cut off to line foxholes or as souvenirs, the insides being cannibalized by troops or locals, and destruction by the enemy or by the glider pilots themselves to prevent the enemy taking control of the glider and its contents.

---

56 Office of Flying Safety, Headquarters AAF, "Pilot Training Manual for the CG-4A Glider," 1945.
57 School of Applied Tactics, "Troop Carrier Aviation," Captain Wasson J. Wilson, AC, (200-4-14-L), (201-4- 4-L), (202-4-14-L), (243-4-14-L), Tactical Center, Orlando, Florida, Troop Carrier Division, Combat Operations Department, Dec. 3, 1943, 7.
58 Mrazek, *Fighting Gliders*, 155-57. To "pick up" a glider, two poles were stood on end a good distance apart and a glider towrope slung between them. A C-47 flew low overhead and seized the rope with its tow hook. The rope unraveled and the glider, which was hooked on the other end, would be airborne at speeds of 120 mph within seconds.

THE PILOT

When the glider program was first introduced, both the Army and the Air Corps arms of the Army Air Corps vied for control of the program and the men assigned to it. The Army held that since the glider pilots were transporting infantry into combat situations, they should receive the same training as the troops they carried and, upon landing, assume the role of combat soldiers.[59] The Air Corps insisted, on the other hand, that all pilots belonged to them, and in the final outcome, they did retain control. The inability of the two commands to compromise severely handicapped the glider pilots' infantry training.

In its Directive of 1942, the Air Corps stated that combat training was to be secondary to flight training, based solely on their supposition that "the glider pilot will participate in ground combat only in exceptional circumstances or after his glider has been wrecked in landing."[60] This was contradicted by the 1943 Confidential Report on Troop Carrier Aviation: "Even though they are to be evacuated as soon as possible, glider pilots are given training in ground tactics so they can join with glider troops until evacuated."[61] Unfortunately for the glider pilots, the ground training was not always adequate, and both the "exceptional circumstances" and crashed glider criteria were met all too often. Although not all gliders were damaged on landing, many pilots did controlled landings; anti-glider obstacles, small landing fields, and hot landing zones resulted in wrecked gliders on almost every mission.

---

59 The British, German, and Soviet glider pilot regiments were set up along these lines. Only the United States attached their glider pilots to the Air Corps rather than the Army.

60 Brig. Gen. L. S. Kuter, Memo for the Air Force Director of Individual Training (hereafter referred to as AFRIT), May 12, 1942 in Air Adjutant General (hereafter referred to as AAG) 211 A, "Officers, Titles and Grades," quoted in Assistant Chief of Air Staff, Intelligence, Historical Division, "Army Air Forces Historical Studies: No. 1: The Glider Pilot Training Program 1941 to 1943" (hereafter referred to as "AAF Historical Studies: No. 1"), September 1943, 20.

61 AAF School of Applied Tactics, Captain Wasson J. Wilson, "Troop Carrier Aviation," Troop Carrier Division Combat Operations Department, AAF Tactical Center, Orlando, Fla., Dec. 3, 1943. 7.

Anti-glider obstacles on the landing zones could be expected by the first few glider serials flying into enemy territory. Obstacles such as "Rommel's asparagus"—telephone poles, iron posts, or stripped tree trunks strung with barbed wire or ropes—were the most commonly used. They reflected German innate knowledge of glider vulnerabilities and ingenuity and inflicted severe damage to the gliders and men forced to land in fields planted with them. Set twelve to fifteen feet apart across an entire landing field, they prevented gliders from passing between them, damaging their wings and detonated if they were attached to mines. If German supplies and time were short, trees edging the LZs were stripped of bark and leaves and were used in lieu of poles.

This glider landed in a field in Normandy near St. Mere Eglise planted with "Rommel's asparagus," nicknamed for the German General Erwin Rommel. Notice the spacing of the poles, which would not allow a glider to pass through two poles unscathed. What look like telephone

lines or power lines, another major hazard is visible to the left of the photo. This glider had both wings broken off; one is visible on the left side of the glider just in front of the tail, and the plexiglass on the cockpit appears to have collapsed or the cockpit broke off. It does not look as though the cargo was unloaded. Behind the hedgerow in the next field are other gliders. The glider may have landed in this field for any number of reasons; often smoke obscured the field, the pilot had to cut off, the towplane cut him off a bit too early, or his plane was damaged. Photo courtesy of Silent Wings Museum.

This CG-4A with its cockpit raised landed on a landing zone lightly planted with "Rommel's asparagus," which the glider's left wing has come in contact with it. This picture was shot in Southern France, Operation DRAGOON. This glider landed relatively intact, as did the gliders behind it. The loading ramps can be clearly seen, as can the raised cockpit. Photo Courtesy of Silent Wings Museum.

Tanks routinely operated on the same type of terrain that was utilized for glider landings; therefore, tank traps were often encountered. They served a dual purpose, disabling armored vehicles and destroying gliders.[62] Flight Officers Taylor and McDonough landed their glider on the same field as used by American tanks, which added to the chaos and presented another element of danger—burning tanks on the field:

> No trouble in flight, arrived at drop zone ok, 6 minutes late into drop zone couldn't find field & cracked up glider, ran into a hole, swung around between two tanks that were burning (american tanks) only saw one man with leg shot off. 7 men, I and co-pilot were all landed okay. . . . after landing glider caught fire from the burning tanks. Next the mortar fire hit the glider and it exploded & burned up. Machine gun fire to heavy to unload supplies. . . . F/O Talty, F/O Buchan, F/O Mack broken legs and scratches.[63]

American paratroopers were usually dropped in advance of the glider missions, one of their objectives being to clear the landing zones of the enemy and the obstacles. Despite their best efforts, this could not always be done for any number of reasons. Many times, the Germans were still in control when the first few waves of gliders arrived. For the flights that landed in the midst of the battle, some active involvement in combat was inevitable, whether it was unloading the glider under fire, aiding the airborne in clearing the area for the next wave of gliders, or simply struggling for self-preservation. A small reading of returning glider pilot reports gives

---

62 Tank traps were sharply angled declines dug into the ground, with dirt piled up at the end to form a ten- to fourteen-foot wall. The idea was for the tank to hit the decline and continue rolling forward until it collided with the embankment. The tanks could not extricate themselves and were blown up by the enemy.
63 F/O John A. Taylor and F/O John McDonough, "Glider Pilot Interrogation," 437th TCG, 83rd TCS, Mission Reports, RG 18 Entry #7, Federal Records Center, Suitland, Md.

insight into conditions on the ground when the gliders arrived:

> Upon landing we were under small arms fire. I was pinned in the glider about 15 minutes but A/B got out quickly. The Germans started closing in on us and using concussion grenades. We got out of the glider in a hurry and were forced to leave all our equipment. We started west through the woods having to shoot our way out.[64]

> My glider was the 11th to take off. Over our flight to the DZ was very good but had to cut off too high. After release, everything on the ground opened up on us. We were hit by small arms fire while in the air. After landing snipers zeroed on the door of gliders. Three men hit hard while leaving glider, left only two of us able to fight. We were pinned down for about 45 minutes then the two of us went over and took the house where the sniper was hiding.[65]

> Lts. Chesher and Friedman tow-plane cut - off, tail shot off and control of ship was getting difficult as we could feel fabric ripping. F/O Russell was met near Gourbesville, but because of my injuries received during flight and crash landing (laceration, flak wounds leg and shoulder) received during flight and crash landing I was unable to go on with him. Was forced to leave that area next morning because the enemy moved in, in force. Was with an airborne infantryman. While evading enemy patrols, and attempting to get back to our forces I was wounded by sniper fire in the left forearm and by machine gun fire in left hip. Was captured by German patrol

---

64 2nd Lt. Dan W. Hoffpauir and 2nd Lt. Carl G. Belville, "TCMICS-GP," Operation Varsity, 439th TCG, 93rd TCS, RG18 Entry #7, Federal Records Center, Suitland, Md.

65 2nd Lt. Alfred A. Pate, "TCMGICS," 440th TCG, 95th TCS, Varsity Mission 3/45, RG18 Entry #7, Federal Records Center, Suitland, Md.

enroute to a C.P. (was headed for bridge at La Fierre to see in whose hands that town was in). [66]

We carried 53 rounds of 105mm ammo and 3 A/B. Upon landing we were under intensive SA [small arms] fire. We hit the ground quickly. A/B and Lt. Sullivan immediately returned fire Sullivan was wounded within one minute after getting out of glider. We took cover as best we could. Sullivan asked for help and I tried to get to him, but was unable to do so because of intense fire. A/B from another glider tried to throw a smoke grenade, but instead threw a phosphorous and set fire to his glider. When the glider caught fire we made a dash for a hedge 30 yards away. Sullivan couldn't move but all the rest of us got to the hedge. We were pinned down there until darkness. On several occasions we tried to get to Sullivan but the fire was too intense. He started to crawl but was too weak to make fast progress. He was fired on several times and finally reached us at 1800A. I gave him first aid and soon after dark we started to move out. I carried him on my back for about 30 yards, but his bandages came off and we decided it would be better to leave him. Sullivan showed a lot of courage and was an inspiration to all of us. . . . I sent two A/B to look for a stretchers and an aid man. They returned and I led the patrol back to Sullivan and the wounded A/B.[67]

Flight Officer George F. Brennan discovered that they were off course, and as he approached a small field for landing, he encountered a German anti-aircraft battery. "I thought we were done," he stated

---

66   Untitled Invasion of Normandy Handwritten Narrative, RG 18 Entry #7, 437th TCG, Federal Records Center, Suitland Md. The unidentified author of this report was captured by Germans for a period of time before he wrote it. He flew with F/O Edward H. Russell.
67   Lt. Thomas L. Sullivan and Lt. Harry N. Colby, "TCMICS-GP," RG 18, Entry #7, 95th TCS, Mission Reports, Federal Records Center, Suitland, Md.

in an interview with Ed Keyes for an article in *On Tow* after the war. Ed Keyes recounted Brennan's horrific experience:

> Brennan's left foot was smashed by a shell fragment and another ripped through his left hand. A third struck him in the chest and a fourth hit him in the left side of the neck, smashed through his jaw and exited below his right ear. . . . A paratrooper, Sergeant Brasel Thompson, sitting in the copilot's seat took a fragment through the hip. It passed through his groin and exited the opposite hip.[68]

Brenan relayed his memory of the flight and its aftermath:

> I'll never know how I got that glider down; by the grace of God, I guess. We skidded in flames into a field, and I told everyone to scatter before the Germans got us. We made it into a nearby ditch. I kept passing out and coming to. My jaw was hurting pretty bad. It was a mess. What really scared me was the hole in my chest. Blood was bubbling out and I thought I had been hit in the lungs. Turned out I hadn't. Then a German patrol found the glider. We could see they were SS troops from their black uniforms. Thompson had his M-1 rifle and I had a sub machine gun with four clips. If I had kept still they probably wouldn't have found me but I was damned mad that I had been shot up and I was probably as good as dead. I figured right then and there I was going to extract a price for dying. We opened up on the patrol and killed them all. I'm not sure but there must have been 12 or 15 men. We fired all the ammo we had. We knew we had to find another place to hole up. We had no idea how far we were from our guys. . .With

---

[68] Ed Keyes, "The Glider Pilots Rogue Gallery," *ON TOW or The Angle of the Dangle*, Vol. III, No II, National World War II Glider Pilots Association, (June 1988):14-15.

Thompson dragging me we made it to a barn and of all the damn barns in Holland, we picked one that belonged to a Nazi sympathizer... A German army officer showed up, a captain I think he was. He had some men with him and they tried to question us. I'll say one thing, that officer was a gentleman. He gave us first aid and tried to make us comfortable. Then he told the Dutch woman we would soon be dead, so he and his men took our watches and cigarette lighters and left. I had passed out again. The next thing I knew someone was kicking me hard in the ribs. In fact, every rib on that side was broken. It was an SS officer with two men. He stuck his face down in mine and demanded to know where I had been scheduled to land, I was still mad, and I hurt like hell, so I made some comment like, 'In the middle of Berlin.' It was a dumb thing to do. He kicked me in the head with those heavy jackboots he wore and fractured my skull. It's a wonder they didn't shoot us on the spot. Finally, the officer left, but his men remained to guard us. They apparently thought we were as good as dead, so they got lax and pretty soon dozed off. Thompson had two knives hidden on him and we decided to go for the sentries. We crept up and knifed both of them. Then with Thompson dragging me, we made our way across the barnyard. We hadn't gotten far when a voice called out for us to halt. It was a young Dutch farmer who turned out to be a member of the underground."[69]

Brennan woke up in a Catholic Hospital in the town of Schijndel. The nuns had to hide him in plain sight because the elite corps of the German military, the Schutzstaffel, also known as the SS, made rounds through the wards. To disguise him, they dressed him as pregnant woman on the maternity ward. It turned out to be a

---

69 Ed Keyes, "The Glider Pilots Rogue Gallery," *ON TOW or The Angle of the Dangle*, 14-15.

blessing that he had his jaw wired shut since he could not answer any questions directed to him from the German SS. The nuns thought the SS would get suspicious if he lingered in the maternity ward for the eight weeks he was there, so they moved him to a private ward and placed a TB sign on his door.[70] The author, Ed Keyes, also a former glider pilot, went on to state, Brennan "lays claim to the distinction of 'being the only man to crash land a fiery glider with only one hand, one leg and one eye and live to tell about it.'"[71]

For others, making it to the command post as ordered was not always as impossible as it was for Flight Officer Brennan, but the difficulty in following this directive was compounded by the fact that glider pilots were not always issued maps or compasses and the command post was not always in the briefed location. Many comments, such as the following, reflect the glider pilot's frustrations.

> "Better maps and photographs - definite place to report, as CP was not definitely located in briefing."[72]

As late as September of 1944, the time of Operation Market Garden, glider pilots were still requesting basic aids and currency.

> . . . glider pilots advocated that they be equipped with the following aids in addition to those aids regularly issued 1. Invasion money and aid kits 2. Maps leading to the LZ and a detailed map of the LZ. Maps of the route are needed in case of a forced landing before the LZ is reached. Glider pilots should also be given ample time to study maps before briefing. A photo of the LZ area for detailed study before the mission.[73]

---

70 Keyes, "The Glider Pilots Rogue Gallery," 14-15.
71 Keyes, "The Glider Pilots Rogue Gallery," 14.
72 F/O Leslie H. Luedtke, "TCMICS-GP," GIS 313th TCG 89th TCS, 313th GP-SU, Federal Records Center, Suitland, Md.
73 "Market," September 44, 313th TCG, RG 18 Entry #7, 62, Federal Records Center, Suitland, Md.

Command posts were also under attack or at times chaotic. Lt. Cobb acted as copilot in his glider. He remained at the glider while the pilot, Lt. Appleman, made a reconnaissance of the grounds. It was dark at the time. When Lt. Appleman did not show back up, Cobb and the airborne waited until noon the following day. During this time, they were surrounded by Germans and found themselves in skirmishes. While trying to avoid the enemy locating them, Cobb and one other were separated from the rest of the airborne infantry he had hauled in. They were fired upon from all sides and were forced to hide in ditches for the next four and a half days and travel only at night. At one point, the German troops heard them in in the hedgerows and fired at them. The Germans were so well dug in everywhere, Cobb stated, "it seemed impossible to go further," so they changed direction. Once again, they "ran into more Jerries and they seemed thicker than ever." They ended up sheltering in a French dairy barn and were fed and cared for at great risk to the family that owned it. When the Americans were closer, they left and went through heavy fighting to reach the American lines.[74]

The battlefields were a dynamic situation; at times glider pilots made it to the command post but found so much chaos there, they ended up staying with the airborne they carried in their gliders. During the invasion of Normandy, Flight Officers Laverne M. Smith and John F. Lawton with their airborne passengers reported to their command post with the jeep and 57mm gun unloaded from the British Horsa glider they flew in. There was so much confusion at the command post, the glider pilots and the airborne hauled the gun to the crossroads as the airborne had been briefed. The glider pilots then operated with the airborne guarding the crossroads that night, knocking out an approaching tank the next morning. They picked up two lost paratroopers, demolished a machine gun nest, and defended the road until American tanks arrived. When they went back to town, they were under "heavy barrage" and could only

---

74   Lt. Walter L. Cobb and 2nd Lt. Stratton M. Appleman, 437th TCG, RG 18 Entry#7, Federal Records Center, Suitland, Md.

make their way to the division command post after it lifted.[75]

The need for combat training was evident to those fighting in the ETO. Numerous report summaries were sent to headquarters from all levels of command, stressing its importance, but no change in the pilots' ground training resulted. More critical of the Army Air Forces than the glider pilots, Brigadier General James M. Gavin submitted a report to Major General P. L. Williams of IX Troop Carrier Command (TCC), following Operation MARKET-GARDEN. His comments were a direct reflection of the Army Air Forces' complacency regarding the glider pilots' combat readiness.

> In looking back over the past weeks operations one of the outstanding things in my opinion, and the thing in most urgent need of correction, is the method of handling our glider pilots. I do not believe there is anyone in the combat area more eager and anxious to do the correct thing and yet so completely, individually and collectively, incapable of doing it than our glider pilots.
>
> Despite their individual willingness to help, I feel that they were definitely a liability to me. Many of them arrived without blankets, some without rations and water, and a few improperly armed and equipped. They lacked organization of their own because of, they stated, frequent transfer from one Troop Carrier Command unit to another. Despite the instructions that were issued to them to move via command channels to Division Headquarters, they frequently became involved in small unit actions to the extent that satisfied their passing curiosity, or simply left to visit nearby towns. In an airborne operation where, if properly planned, the first few hours are the quietest, this can be very harmful, since all units

---

75   F/Os LaVergne M. Smith and F/O John F. Lawton, Untitled After Action Report, 437th TCG, 83rd TCS, Serial 30, Formation No. 11 Horsa Glider, RG18 Entry #7, Federal Records Center, Suitland Md.

tend to [lose] control because of the many people wandering about aimlessly, improperly equipped, out of uniform, and without individual or unit responsibilities. When the enemy reaction builds up and his attack increases in violence and intensity, the necessity for every man to be on the job at the right place, doing his assigned task, is imperative. At this time glider pilots without unit assignment and improperly trained, aimlessly wandering about cause confusion and generally get in the way and have to be taken care of.

In this division, glider pilots were used to control traffic, to recover supplies from the L.Z.s, guard prisoners, and finally were assigned a defensive role with one of the regiments at a time when they were badly needed.

I feel very keenly that the glider pilot problem at the moment is one of our greatest unsolved problems. I believe now that they should be assigned to airborne units, take training with the units and have a certain number of hours allocated periodically for flight training. I am also convinced that our airborne unit copilots should have flight training so as to be capable of flying the glider if the pilot is hit.[76]

Again, the Army and the Air Corps were in conflict. What the Air Corps had refused to provide in combat training, Gavin's last lines imply by the words "periodic flight training"; the Army would be as reticent about providing in-flight training, yet both were an integral part of an average mission for the glider pilots. Operation MARKET-GARDEN served as a catalyst for many other letters such as Gavin's. Major Hugh Nevins recognized that some of the glider pilots did not have previous combat experience and recommended additional infantry training for all:

---

76 Brig. Gen. James M. Gavin, Letter to Major General P.L. Williams IX TCC, Sept. 25, 1944, 4, RG 18 Entry #7, Federal Records Center, Suitland, Md.

> Basic infantry training should be intensified for glider pilots. Use of cover, camouflage, types of foxholes, slit trenches, etc., best suited for protection against strafing and shelling, range estimation, scouting and patrolling are probably the most urgent subjects. No criticism is made of the glider pilots under the control of the undersigned during ground action subsequent to operation 'MARKET.' Said glider pilots excited the admiration and respect of all A/B commanders who worked with them, including the Commanding General and G-3 of the Division. It is believed, however, that glider pilots without previous combat experience, might benefit by the above recommended training.[77]

Even the glider pilots themselves recommended organization based on infantry lines. The Glider Pilot Interrogation Reports reflect their recommendations based on their firsthand experiences. Flight Officer Clarence Locke was still advocating for further organization of the glider pilots to make them more effective upon landing as late as Operation VARSITY. Locke suggested,

> Consideration should be given to practicability of having GPs organized to operate as squads with infantry squad weapons.[78]

Despite the combat training the later glider pilot recruits received, there was still a need for more, as expressed by Lt. Emory Rhodes, again in Operation VARSITY:

---

[77] Major Hugh J. Nevins to Colonel G.M. Jones IX TCC, "Recommendations," October 1, 1944, Folder 546.452K, 1-2. Air Force Historical Research Agency, Maxwell AFB.

[78] F/O Clarence Locke and F/O John H. Liska, "TCMCS-GP," 437th TCG, G.P.s Attached and Assigned to 85th TCS, RG 18 Entry #7, Federal Records Center, Suitland Md.

> Glider pilots should be impressed with the need to follow infantry tactics, such as hitting the ground promptly.[79]

The comments at the time of Varsity were reflective of the need for more integration with the airborne troops that existed in the earlier missions. Flight Officer Wescoat stated in his report following his return from Operation MARKET-GARDEN,

> If G.P. are going to serve as front line infantry men give them some infantry training - closer work with A/B before missions.[80]

This would have been the most logical decision, considering that once behind enemy lines, the glider pilots were, for all intents and purposes, on their own until their arrival back at their home bases and on the front lines.

The glider pilot's isolation from operating as part of a group was exacerbated by their frequent detached service to other troop carrier squadrons or groups. The 314th Troop Carrier Group glider pilots were a prime example. Some of the first glider pilots, such as glider pilot Lt. Col. Paul Mousseau, were assigned to the 314th at the beginning of the war. It was not until the last mission of the war, Varsity, that the 314th TCG actually towed any gliders on a mission. Instead, the 314th Troop Carrier Group glider pilots were on "detached service" to other units for missions up until that time.

Glider pilots were also placed on detached service if other TCG or TCS needed additional manpower. Once the mission or duty was completed, they were pulled back and "attached" back to their originally assigned unit. Consequently, they did not necessarily know, and were not known by, the flight crews that would be towing them to the LZ. Sometimes they didn't know the copilot (if one was

---

79 1st Lt. Emory Rhodes, "TCMICS-GP," 437th TCG 84thTCS, RG18 Entry #7, 437th Interrogation Sheets, Varsity, Federal Records Center, Suitland, Md.
80 F/O William L. Wescoat, "TCMICS-GP," 61st TCG 59th TCS, 61st TCG HI/SU. Air Force Historical Research Agency, Maxwell, AFB.

assigned to them). The glider pilots often were unknown entities new to a group or squadron they were flying into battle with and whose skills, experiences, and personalities were unknown to those members as well. As Flight Officer Clifford W. Tilley stated,

> Don't like this DS [Detached Service] business. Prefer to fly with my own buddies. Copilot never flew a glider before.[81]

The fact that glider pilots carried out an extremely hazardous role in World War II cannot be argued. Unlike any other, their mission demanded precise flying skills combined with a strong survival instinct to make up for what they lacked in training. The lack of organization and forethought put into the employment of the glider pilot after landing and between missions is evident, was known, and, like the majority of the program's problems, stemmed from its recruitment and training practices.

The AAF's preoccupation with setting and meeting recruitment quotas at the expense of other crucial preparation was responsible for the confusion connected with the glider pilots' duties, qualifications, and prescribed role in combat. The territorial tug of war between the Army and Air Forces' ground and air commanders resulted in deficiencies that carved the glider pilot into what he had to become to survive—a lone, exceedingly independent and resourceful individual. For them, it was not a matter of reputation; it was a matter of survival and covering their own backs.

---

81   F/O Clifford W. Tilley 437thTCG 84th TCS, "TCMCS-GP," RG 18 Entry#7, Serial A-8, GPs Assigned and Attached 84th TCS, Federal Records Center, Suitland, Md.

CHAPTER 3

THE EVOLUTION OF THE GLIDER PILOT

"The American glider pilots were a mixed bag: flunked out aviation cadets; men who were too old for flight crew training or who could not pass the strict physical examination; ground troops who wished to get into the Air Corps; men who wanted adventure, wanted to try something new - and, above all, to fly."

—Milton Dank, *The Glider Gang*

Perhaps the greatest injustice to the glider pilots is the perpetuation of generalized statements about their qualifications and skill. Broad generalized statements that encompass the entire four years of the program create the impression of washed-out old men who couldn't see well enough to fly but were too cantankerous to retire. Such assertions reflect only a small portion of the misconceptions that surround the glider pilots of World War II. Too often, the complexity and utter confusion of the recruitment procedures were to blame for the inability of those both involved in and distanced from the program to discern glider pilots' qualifications and exactly what their role in combat was.

When the program originated, it was the intention of the planners to train power pilots as glider pilots, thereby allowing them to serve a dual purpose. Following a series of revisions in acceptance criteria, pilots with a variety of qualifications were eventually accepted. It was only when the United States entered the war that the Air Corps realized it could not spare its power pilots to cross-train. Consequently, the program was opened to civilians who met the required standards. Although the flight curriculum was adapted to the level of experience of entering pilots, the same cannot be said of the combat training. It was not until 1943 that a curriculum setting the basic combat training standards for all aviation students was established and adhered to.[1]

Those who transferred into the glider program from another branch of service had already received basic training. The *civilian* volunteers, entering directly into the Air Corps, received no military training except for the few hours allotted to physical education classes by the civilian instructors in the soaring schools. The first classes of graduating glider pilots were not to receive any real form of combat training until they arrived at their overseas command posts. The quality and quantity of this training was very subjective, dependent upon the TCG and ultimately the TCS to which they were assigned. Still, the Air Corps did not seriously address the issue until faced with enormous training delays caused by glider manufacturing problems. Due to the shortage of gliders and the limited number of students, a backlog of students awaiting training built up. The morale of the 10,000 or so students in the glider pools had reached its lowest ebb, and serious disciplinary problems had begun when a combat training program was finally considered. The program was contemplated more for its ability to fill the time and appease the men than for its obvious merits in a combat situation. Upon the completion of a study, in which all the available facilities and supplies were found inadequate, the plan was abandoned. It was not until late April of 1943 that TCC stepped forward and assumed the responsibility for the glider pilots' infantry training.

---

[1] Note: "aviation students" refers to those enrolled in the Glider Pilot Program, while "aviation cadets" refers to those in the Power Pilot Program. To further reduce confusion the Recruitment and Training programs will be referred to as under the AAC, although the program began under the AAC and operated and ended under the United States Army Air Forces (USAAF) when the AAC ceased to have its own autonomy as of February 28, 1942.

RECRUITMENT

The first Experimental Glider Pilot Program was instituted in February of 1941. The glider mission was defined as "transporting personnel and materiel and seizing objectives that can not normally be reached by conventional ground units."[2] It consisted of twelve power pilots who were cross-trained to be utilized as instructors when the program expanded. On July 7, 1941, the 12 Glider Pilot Program was succeeded with the 150 Glider Pilot Program, and necessary contracts were signed with a civilian soaring school for training.[3] It is significant that at this time no tactical use for the glider had been established, nor had the number of troopers each glider was to carry into battle been calculated; yet it was upon these figures that the final number of pilots recruited was supposed to be based. Consequently, as the glider's capabilities became more apparent, the military commands foresaw a continuing need for additional pilots. With the limited training capabilities of the soaring schools and the small number of gliders available, the ever-increasing quotas were unrealistic.

On January 23, 1942, the Air Corps Flying Training Command (FTC) was established.[4] It was responsible for the individual training of the glider pilots and, for the next two years, dictated numerous revisions in the training curriculum. Its primary focus, however, was always on flight training. Shortly after its establishment, the first large-scale recruitment efforts began. Lt. Ed Cook, a former glider pilot instructor, recounted his experience.

---

2   Assistant Chief of Air Staff, Intelligence, Historical Division, "Army Air Forces Historical Studies: No. 1," September 1943, Air Force Historical Research Agency, Maxwell AFB, 4.
3   Assistant Chief of Air Staff, Intelligence, Historical Division, "Army Air Forces Historical Studies: No. 1," September 1943, Bolling AFB Historical Research Library, Washington, D.C., 7.
4   Adjutant General (hereafter referred to as AG), 322.2 (1-4-42) MR-M-AAF/A-1, Jan. 23, 1942, quoted in Assistant Chief of Air Staff, "AAF Historical Studies: No. 1," 13.

As you will soon find out there was little formalization in the establishment of flying curriculum in the glider program. I was selected as an instructor when I completed the so called "advanced" glider training at Lockbourne AFB, Ohio and sent to Starkville, Miss. to start instructing "B" students in TG-5 training gliders. . . Little more than a month later, I was instructing truly "advanced" gliders at Stuttgart, Ark. in CG-4A's. My total Army time by then as a Staff Sergeant Pilot was about 1 month of "basic" training, 5 or 6 weeks of "deadstick" training in Taylorcraft L-2's in Minnesota and 2 weeks at Lockbourne flying basic sailplanes. I had my first flight in a CG-4A with maybe 15 minutes "stick" time when I took my first student up. We had received no outlines or procedures. Just to make pilots out of them. . . . I had gone into the service as a licensed private pilot, the reason I received so little flying time before starting as an instructor.[5]

Shortly after, the Flying Training Commands establishment the first large-scale recruitment efforts began. On February 19, 1942, the 1,000 Glider Pilot Program was announced. Initially, only qualified Army Air Corps Flying School pilots were to be accepted. This was "due to the large amount of skill believed to be necessary to pilot gliders at night under instrument conditions and to land them in small fields."[6] Prior to its formal announcement, the AAC realized that it could not spare its pilots to cross-train for the glider program. Instead, it recommended that pilots be selected from among Civilian Pilot Training (CPT) school graduates. On December 31, 1941, it was decided that volunteers would be accepted in the following order:

---

5   Lt. Edward L. Cook, WWII Glider Pilot Instructor, Former National Chairman Executive Council, National World War II Glider Pilots Association, letter to Monique Taylor, August 30,1989.
6   Assistant Chief of Air Staff, "AAF Historical Studies: No. l," 11.

1. Power plane pilots who have had the CAA [Civil Aeronautics Association] Secondary Course
2. Power plane pilots who have had the CAA Primary Course
3. Glider pilots who have had at least thirty hours glider time[7]

The physical requirements remained rigid, the same as those in Air Corps power pilot training, and rank was added as an additional inducement to join a dangerous occupation. Newly recruited aviation students entered with enlisted status and were promoted to at least staff sergeant upon graduation from the program.[8] The AAC also issued a statement pertaining to the preferred background of the applicants, which should "come from the Combat Arms inasmuch as they should function as a member of the Combat Team upon landing."[9] This is in complete contradiction to their later statements.

The projected number of glider pilots needed in the war effort was increased to 4,200 on April 1, 1942.[10] An amendment stating the preference for Twin-Engine Advanced Pilot Course military graduates over other applicants was followed by additional changes to the entrance requirements two days later.[11] The revisions required all glider pilot trainees to be enlisted graduates of the Air Force Advanced Flying Schools, which was in direct conflict with the recruitment policy of the 1,000 Glider Pilot Program. The students who had been accepted and scheduled for training from the Civil Aeronautics Association (CAA) were replaced. The abrupt shift

---

7   Assistant Chief of Air Staff, "AAF Historical Studies: No. 1," 12.
8   This was a substantial jump in rank and pay grade. See appendix A for Officers' and Enlisted ranks.
9   Routing & Record Sheet (hereafter referred to as R&R), Office Chief of Air Corp to Chief of Air Staff (hereafter referred to as C/AS), Dec. 31, 1941, in AAG 353.9 A, Glider Training, quoted in Assistant Chief of Air Staff, "AAF Historical Studies: No. 1," 12.
10 Assistant Chief of Air Staff, "AAF Historical Studies: No. 1," 14.
11 Commanding General (hereafter referred to as CG), AAF to CG, Army Air Forces Flying Training Command (hereafter referred to as AAFFTC), April 1, 1942, in AAG 353.9 3A Glider Training, quoted in Assistant Chief of Air Staff, "AAF Historical Studies: No. 1," 15.

in policy was based on the size of the gliders being produced as well as additional foreseeable duties of the pilots: the nine- and fifteen-passenger gliders were approximately the same size as a B-18 airplane, whereas the thirty-passenger gliders had wing spans larger than the B-17 bomber. Additionally, the glider pilots would be required to double as tow pilots and fly under night and instrument conditions.[12] The dual role of glider pilots never materialized, although the tow pilots did, some unhappily, substitute for glider pilots on a few combat missions.[13]

Eight days after the announcement limiting candidacy to Air Force pilot graduates, and the cancellation of the selected civilian pilots' training, the decision to transfer 4,200 enlisted pilots was reversed. The AAC reported that they could not be spared for the program. In order to make up for lost volunteers, the flying requirements were again altered to resemble those of the 1,000 Glider Pilot Program. Volunteers had to meet one of the following conditions: be a graduate of either the Civilian Pilot Training (CPT) Secondary Course (the Primary Course was no longer acceptable), hold or have held at least a private Airman Certificate with a 0-240 horsepower or a 2 S rating (service rating), or be a glider pilot with thirty hours or two hundred flights. The minimum age for entrance into the program was lowered to eighteen and extended to thirty-two.[14] This was true for all AAC pilot programs, glider and power.

On May 8, 1942, there was a third major increase in the glider pilot quota. Approximately two months after the 1,000 Glider Pilot Program, and thirty-eight days after the 4,200 Glider Pilot Program,

---

12   AFRIT to CG, AAFFTC, April 3, 1942, in MG 353.9 3A, Glider Training, quoted in Assistant Chief of Air Staff, "AAF Historical Studies: No. 1," 15.
13   Glider pilots copiloted transport planes between missions, yet, despite AAF promises to the contrary, regardless of how many hours they flew, the AAF would not count these hours toward a power pilot rating because they were accumulated during wartime. Lt. Col. Paul W. Mousseau (USAF Ret.), interview by author, 20 June 1989, Fresno, California.
14   AFRIT to C/AS, April 11, 1942, in AAG 353.9 3A, Glider Training, quoted in Assistant Chief of Air Staff, "AAF Historical Studies: No. 1," 15-16.

the 6,000 Glider Pilot Program was announced. The increased recruitment objective of 1,800 pilots was in addition to those who had yet to be signed up under the 4,200 Glider Pilot Program. These rapid changes called for the increased recruitment and graduation of the volunteers within a shortened time frame. In response to the time limitations, another revision of qualifications took place. In order to meet the newest quota, male graduates of the CPT and citizens of the US were made eligible. Also qualified were holders of a private CAA Airman Certificate or higher and former CAA pilots, providing their licenses had not been invalidated for more than two years. All applicants had to be between eighteen and thirty-five years of age.[15] Three days later, the program announced the acceptance of "former aviation cadets or aviation students to apply if they had been eliminated for flying deficiency after having successfully completed the Elementary phase of instruction."[16]

After the 6,000 Glider Pilot Program was put into effect, the first formal definition of the glider pilot's combat role was passed along to the Flying Training Command and the training centers. Brigadier General L. S. Kuter, in a memo to AFRIT dated May 12, 1942, stated,

> In training glider pilots, primary attention will be given to their training in the piloting role. The secondary function of these pilots ... will consist of ground combat operations with the airborne units which have been transported in their gliders.
>
> It is expected that the glider pilot will receive the majority of his ground combat training in conjunction with the mass training of air-borne troops in gliders. Ground combat training will be included as a secondary phase of his glider pilot training only to such extent as will not interfere with his training as a pilot.

---

15 CAS to CG, AAFFTC, May 8, 1942, in AAG 353.9 3A, Glider Training, quoted in Assistant Chief of Air Staff, "AAF Historical Studies: No. 1," 18.
16 Lt. Col. A. S. Barnhart to CG, AAFFTC, May 11, 1942, in AAG 353.9 A, Glider Training, quoted in Assistant Chief of Air Staff, "AAF Historical Studies: No. 1," 18.

> The role of the glider pilot in combat will be primarily to land his glider safely, expedite the rapid debarkation of his passengers, secure his glider on the ground, assure that transport which may land after the glider-borne troops have secured the airdrome or locality to permit reinforcement by transport-borne troops. The glider pilot will participate in ground combat only in exceptional circumstances or after his glider has been wrecked in landing.[17]

The memo contradicted earlier statements referring to the glider pilot as "a member of a combat team" and was to contradict later statements of the Airborne Command regarding the inevitability of the glider pilots' involvement in combat.

The FTC was still short 3,600 volunteers. To attract them, an extensive publicity campaign was launched with the Civil Aeronautics Administration—85,000 Airman Certificate holders were sent circulars describing the glider program.[18] Two days later, additional pamphlets were sent to all posts in the continental United States, urging men to volunteer. Applicants were qualified if they either held a current or lapsed Airman Certificate (providing it had not lapsed prior to January 1, 1942) or had completed 200 or more glider flights. In direct conflict with the 4,200 Glider Pilot Program, power pilot eliminees were no longer accepted. All volunteers had to pass a flying duty physical, and all enlisted men needed to score at least 110 on the Army General Classification Test.[19] The test consisted of three parts: arithmetic reasoning, reading vocabulary, and pattern analysis. The score of 110 was necessary to go to Officers

---

17   Memo for AFRIT by Brig. Gen. L. S. Kuter, May 12, 1942, in AAG 211 A, Officers, Titles and Grades, quoted in Assistant Chief of Air Staff, "AAF Historical Studies: No. 1," 20.
18   Memo for AG by Military Personnel, May 9, 1942, in AAG 353.9 A, Glider Training, quoted in Assistant Chief of Air Staff, "AAF Historical Studies: No. 1," 23.
19   AAF 352, May 11, 1942, quoted in Assistant Chief of Air Staff, "AAF Historical Studies: No. 1," 23.

Candidate School.[20]

The program was still short of its quota. Five days later, on May 16, 1942, flying eliminees were once more accepted, providing they had had at least fifty hours in a military or naval aircraft as either the pilot or student pilot. The acceptable period for a lapsed Airman's Certificate was pushed back to January 1, 1941, and both officers and enlisted men were allowed to train at their present ranks, the enlisted personnel being promoted to the rank of staff sergeant upon completion of the training program.[21] Finally, both officers and enlisted men would receive their glider pilot rating upon graduation, allowing postwar employment within the field.

To further entice possible candidates, it was announced on June 5 that "selected graduates" would be chosen for officers' appointments upon the "Demonstration of soldierly qualities of leadership, judgment, force and discipline . . ."[22] The statement did not reflect that the organizational structure of TCC had a limited number of officers' slots in each squadron. Due to the relative newness of TCC, it is unlikely that this would have been common knowledge at the time.

Despite all efforts made on the part of the AAF, the program was still short of men, and a list of aviation cadets willing to transfer to the glider program was compiled. In a final effort to meet the quota (of which they were short 1,000 men) and make up for the projected attrition rate of 30 percent, the most drastic change in policy to date took place: volunteers with no previous flight experience (Class "B" students) were accepted into the program.[23] On June 10, 1942, the minimal eyesight for Class B volunteers was altered to 20-40,

---

20 Herbert E. Garcia, Lt. Col. (USA), interview with the author, October 24, 1990, Schofield Barracks, HI.
21 AAF 352, May 16, 1942, quoted in Assistant Chief of Air Staff, "AAF Historical Studies: No. 1," 23.
22 AAF 352, June 5, 1942, quoted in Assistant Chief of Air Staff, "AAF Historical Studies: No. 1," 23.
23 Assistant Chief of Air Staff, "AAF Historical Studies: No. 1," 25.

correctable to 20-20 with glasses.[24] To train them, an additional flying program was added that separated Class A and Class B students until a certain level of expertise was reached.[25] To obtain more of the most desirable applicants, the minimum eyesight for Class A students was dropped to 20-100, correctable to 20-20.[26] Although the eyesight was lowered during recruitment periods, in speaking with several veteran glider pilots, not one could recall any co-aviators with poor vision and suggested they may have washed out of the program during training, or worse. Lt. Col. Mousseau explained in a wartime letter to his future wife while he was training in Mobile, Alabama, in 1942 why excellent eyesight was necessary:

> You see the reason they are so strict about eyesight is that you have to fly at night and that takes excellent eyesight, because at night the ground is very deceiving, you may be about twenty feet high and think you are on the ground. When you're flying gliders you have to land the first time around in a powered ship, that is one that has a motor you can always give her the throttle and around again. There were two boys here who wore glasses, they missed the field one night about a week ago, they sent them both home in a pine box.[27]

He further expounded in a subsequent letter on the dangers of night flying even with good eyesight.

> I almost got mine while I was flying nights. I came pretty close to hitting a buddy of mine in midair, it wasn't either of us to

---

24 Air Force Director of Personnel (hereafter referred to as AFDOP), to AG, June 8, 1942, in AAG 353.9 B, Glider Training, quoted in Assistant Chief of Air Staff, "AAF Historical Studies: No. 1," 26.
25 A comparison for these two programs is provided in appendix B.
26 AFDOP to CG, Air Service Command (hereafter referred to as AFASC), July 3, 1942, in AAG 353.9 J, Training in Aviation, Pilot Training, quoted in Assistant Chief of Air Staff, "AAF Historical Studies: No. 1," 28.
27 S/SGT Paul Mousseau to Doris Laferriere, September 8, 1942.

blame, it was the men in the tower who gave me the green light to come in, at the time they didn't see the other ship coming in from the right so we missed each other by about two feet. I was waiting for the crash but it didn't come, thank the lord for that.[28]

The last change under the 6,000 Program allowed enlisted men to enter at the rank of staff sergeant instead of waiting until graduation to be promoted.[29] This, too, was in direct conflict with previous policy, but no effort was made to extend the same privilege to earlier enlisted volunteers.

On August 10, 1942, the final increased quota in the Glider Pilot Program was announced. It called for 7,800 glider pilots by March of 1943 versus the previous 6,000 graduates by July 18, 1943.[30] Barely had the men begun to be recruited when major reductions were put into effect. By the middle of 1943, the recruitment program had far exceeded the number of gliders being produced. In September of 1942, the first reduction was announced. It mandated a 50 percent cut in the number of projected graduates by March of 1943. In numerical terms, this meant 4,000 graduates instead of the 7,800 that had been projected.[31] The sudden reversal in policy was due to difficulties encountered in shipping large quantities of gliders overseas, not in response to the overcrowded conditions in the glider pools. Subsequently, the AAF

---

28 S/SGT Paul Mousseau to Doris Laferriere, October 6, 1942.
29 S/SGT Paul Mousseau to Doris Laferriere, October 6, 1942.
30 Assistant Chief of Air Staff, "AAF Historical Studies: No. 1," 39.
31 Memo for C/AS by A-3, Sept. 25, 1942, in AAG 353.9 3A, Glider Training, quoted in Assistant Chief of Air Staff, "AAF Historical Studies: No. 1," 45.

was left with more pilots than gliders.[32]

In an effort to correct the imbalance, the Preliminary schools were closed down, and the training of all Class B students was terminated regardless of their progress.[33] Additional reductions were sought in December 1943 and January 1944. Trainees who had previously been eliminated from a service flying program had their training discontinued.[34] The Air Corps also began transferring the extra aviation students to other branches of the services. If the volunteer's single objective had been to become a glider pilot, he was given the option of release from the military, although his name would be reregistered with the draft board.[35] Upon completing the disposition of excess personnel, new requirements for glider pilot trainees were drawn up in the event of any future need. The schools were closed down after those who remained in training had graduated. In all, the recruitment program had lasted fifteen months.

The tumultuous start of the Glider Pilot Program led to many false assumptions concerning the general makeup of its pilots. The Army Air Corps had continually set volunteer qualifications to serve their immediate needs with little thought for the future. Taken individually, the glider pilots appeared to possess qualifications that covered the spectrum. On closer investigation, however, this was not the case. The elimination of Class "B" students and aviation cadet washouts from the

---

32 Because the distances precluded any possibility of flight, the gliders were dismantled and packed in crates which, when removed, would serve as living quarters for many of the glider pilots overseas. The fact that after the war people purchased packed gliders merely for the wooden crates, enough to build a good portion of a house, attests to their size. Tragically, the wood was used, and the gliders, very susceptible to the elements, were left to rot. Today, there are a small number of CG-4As in the United States of the approximately 13,000 produced during the war years. All of them are restorations.

33 CG, AAFFTC to CG's, TC's, Oct. 12, 1942, in AAG 360.01 B, Programs, quoted in Assistant Chief of Air Staff, "AAF Historical Studies: No. 1," 45.

34 Daily Diary, AAFFTC, Oct. 16, 1942, quoted in Assistant Chief of Air Staff, "AAF Historical Studies: No. 1," 53.

35 1st Endorsement (CG, AAFFTC to CG, AAF, Feb. 17, 1943), AFRIT to CG, AAFFTC, Feb. 23, 1943, in AAG 221 #2, Pilots, quoted in Assistant Chief of Air Staff, "AAF Historical Studies: No. 1," 64.

program raised the caliber of the glider program's pilots considerably. Due to the long delays between the phases of training, it is possible many of the Class B students with the relaxed vision requirement would not have graduated before the Class B students were discharged from the program. Most men who graduated were either certified glider pilots with a minimum of 200 flights or certified pilots who had at least taken the Preliminary course of the CAA or had some flying experience.[36] When combined with the AAC flight training, the result was highly specialized and qualified pilots.

By the time of graduation and shipping out overseas, the graduated glider pilots were under no illusions of the deadly nature of their occupation. Flight Officer Paul Mousseau relayed the realities of his job, while still Stateside, in a letter dated March 10, 1943:

> One of my best friends and buddy was killed yesterday in a crackup. I helped pick him up and he died in my arms as I carried him to the ambulance. Please don't tell my mother as it will only worry her. We were ten check pilots when we started off and with Hicks getting killed leaves three of us left, all the others were killed within a period of a few months.[37]

COMBAT TRAINING

The FTC set the curriculum for combat instruction in the soaring schools from its beginnings until November of 1942. They were variable at best and, to the knowledge of all commands concerned, ignored. The poor quality of training was not the fault of the soaring schools since they were originally civilian establishments with civilian instructors. They had neither the expertise nor the equipment to

---

36 The acceptance of flight school eliminees preceded that of Class B students in May of 1942. If both groups were eliminated in January 1943, none of them could have been close to graduation. This is especially true, considering the size of the glider pools and that the first glider pilot graduates under the 1,000 Glider Pilot Program entered in December 1941 and graduated in May of 1943.
37 Flight Officer Paul Mousseau to Doris Laferriere, March 10, 1943.

pursue military infantry training.

The Air Corps designation of ground training as secondary to flight training further undermined any attempts at an effective combat program. It was not until November of 1942 that any serious consideration was given to implementing an infantry training program for glider pilots.[38] It was the perfect solution, as far as the Air Corps was concerned, to the disciplinary problems and sagging morale in camps where the students lived for an average of six months, in overcrowded and wretched living conditions, waiting for their final phase of training. Lieutenant Colonel M.A. Quinto of the 88th Glider Infantry Airborne Command researched its feasibility and reported that inadequate facilities at the Advanced training glider pools would prevent the pursuance of any type of combat training program. His recommendations included the following:

> ... that at each of the four Advanced Schools a six weeks' course of instruction consisting of basic military training, small arms, marksmanship, hand grenades, hasty entrenchments, camouflage, map and aerial photography, demolitions, glider-borne tactics, guerilla warfare, night operations, supply and resupply of troops, evacuation, and communications be instituted ... and that an officer from the Airborne Command be assigned to supervise this instruction.[39]

Quinto's report detailing specific needs was one reason for the command's decision that the program was not feasible at that time:

> The program would require an estimated 30 officers and 150 enlisted men as instructors, but worst of all, they would have

---

38   Some of the first graduates were to be sent overseas in approximately January of 1943 after already having been assigned and transferred to their TCG stateside.
39   Lt. Col. M.A. Quinto to CG, Airborne Command, Dec. 17, 1942, in AAG 353.9, Bombardier Training, quoted in Assistant Chief of Air Staff, "AAF Historical Studies: No. 1," 54-55.

no training aids with which to work—no ranges, no bayonet or grenade courses, not even any infantry weapons. The Airborne Command felt that the program exceeded its scope and capabilities.... Moreover, current doctrine did not contemplate the active employment of glider pilots with airborne troops in tactical operations following landings in hostile territory.[40]

A later recommendation by the Airborne Command that the FTC conduct the glider pilots' ground training was met with a negative response. The FTC replied that they would take on no such responsibility.[41] Finally, in February of 1943, a conference was called between the Airborne Command, FTC, and TCC in an attempt to resolve the problem. During the meeting, a statement made by the Airborne Command's representatives clarified their expectations of the glider pilots' role in combat for them to be of use to the command: "[The glider pilot] must be able to function as a member of a combat team; therefore, he should receive training in the ground arms and techniques of the functioning of the combat team."[42] This position conflicted with the earlier AAC statement concluding that the glider pilot need not participate in combat, except under unusual circumstances.

A joint scale maneuver between the glider pilots and the airborne was conducted in December of 1943. The results clearly demonstrated there was no coordinated planning of the duties of both the glider pilots and the airborne once they landed. James Huston, author on US Airborne Operations, summarized it clearly.

> There seemed to be some question again about the training of the glider pilots. One problem which had never been solved

---

40 James Alvin Huston, *Out of the Blue: U.S. Army Airborne Operations in World War II* (West Lafayette, Ind.: Purdue University Studies, 1972), 121.
41 Daily Diary, AFRIT, Jan. 7, 1943, quoted in Assistant Chief of Air Staff, "AAF Historical Studies: No. 1," 55.
42 Assistant Chief of Air Staff, "AAF Historical Studies: No. 1," 56.

satisfactorily was the ground action of the glider pilots after landing. In a major operation the number of glider pilots would be such as to demand some attention. Two hundred leaderless Air Force glider pilots in the midst of ground combat troops could lead to an embarrassing situation. In this maneuver announced plans for the employment of glider pilots as ground troops after landing were not carried out.[43]

Two hundred glider pilots on the ground after a mission was a severe underestimation. It was at this point that Flying Training Command insisted it was responsible only for the individual training of the glider pilot, and by the close of the meeting, TCC was assigned responsibility for the glider pilots' infantry training.[44] Further delays were expected while they formulated a plan. As a result, the glider pilots who had been shipped to Troop Carrier Groups overseas were caught in the overlap. They received the majority of their training either with their Troop Carrier Squadron and the airborne it was transporting or in combat.

On April 3, 1943, TCC commenced training at Bowman Field, Kentucky. They turned the glider pilots who attended into expert soldiers, highly respected by other members of the airborne forces and TCC. The superior training glider pilots received after April 3, 1943, stands in stark contrast to the combat training previous glider pilot graduates received. The new training curriculum consisted of the following:

> The military training, the most extensive yet prescribed, was to include physical training, close order drill, military courtesy and discipline, Air Force and troop carrier organization, care of clothing and equipment, military sanitation and first aid,

---

43 James Alvin Huston, *Out of the Blue: U.S. Army Airborne Operations in World War II*, 138 quoting A-3 Rpt in Report of Combined Maneuver Airborne Troop Carrier Maneuver January 5-9, G-3 Report Mimeo copy in AGF Spl Projects file.
44 Huston, *Out of the Blue*, 138.

marches and bivouacs, arctic, tropical and desert operations, interior guard duty, and defense against the chemical attack. It was also to include individual defense against air and mechanized attack, camouflage, map reading and compass marching, inspections, aircraft identification, and airdrome defense. Training in weapons and marksmanship was to be conducted with the objective of obtaining the highest possible degree of proficiency in the use and care of .30 caliber carbine, .45 caliber submachine gun, .45 caliber automatic pistol, 12-gauge shotgun, .30 caliber rifle, .30 caliber machine gun, .50 caliber machine gun, 60-mm mortar, and 81-mm mortar if practicable.[45]

Compare this with the 314th TCG, 32nd TCS glider pilots' "combat training" on April 21, 1943, just prior to being shipped overseas:

"It was a day of testing, for all the men went on a special march and bivouac in the extensive forests and fields adjoining Fort Benning. This bivouac gave the men an elementary lesson about life in the field. Most of the men of the Squadron, who came from ordinary citizen life, had never had to experience a primitive life in the field."[46]

After a day in the field, they marched back to their base. Their stateside training complete, they were shipped to North Africa.

Surprisingly, all the effort that went into training the remaining glider pilots did nothing to prevent the AAF from sending untrained men on combat missions in the ETO for the duration of the war, when glider pilots were in short supply. In 1945, several power pilots, who had no infantry training or minimal glider training, were

---
[45] Assistant Chief of Air Staff, "AAF Historical Studies: No. 1," 80.
[46] Donald L. Van Reken, *The 32nd Troop Carrier Squadron: An Airborne C-47 Squadron 1942-1945: Pilots, Paratroops and Gliders in North Africa, Sicily, England, France and Germany* (Holland, Mich.: Author, 1989), 13.

ordered to fly gliders into combat.[47] The 1945 Pilot Training Manual for the CG-4A Glider Pilots describes what is needed from a pilot who flies a glider.

> Glider flying calls for no techniques unfamiliar to the power pilot, but it does require a new emphasis on certain old techniques to be a competent glider pilot, for instance, you must be a specialist in landings. The success of any mission depends upon your ability to land your passengers and cargo safely at a given point and time. There are not reserves in an airborne operation. If you fail to deliver your load at the right spot, you may turn a victory into a failure and cause a needless sacrifice of life. . . . Glider flying under conditions encountered in combat demands all the knowledge and skill you can acquire. There are no nearby towns to illuminate the sky at night and no welcome airfields on which to land; high trees may block your approach and rock strewn, stump-studded fields may endanger your landing. The additional hazard of ground fire further complicates the task.[48]

Flight Officer James L. Larkin assigned to the 437th Troop Carrier Group made the following handwritten notes on a copy of his Mission Orders for Operation VARSITY explaining the use of power pilots for the mission and his observations as a glider pilot.

> Most of the copilots in the gliders were bomber & fighter pilot replacements just over from the states - they were assigned as copilots with no glider training whatsoever. Because of

---

47 Their training consisted of approximately four hours of glider instruction compared to the 200 hours-plus that the glider pilots received. Many other power pilots received no training at all. In order to protect these men, Troop Carrier Groups sent them in as copilots with veteran glider pilots. David E. Rosengrants, Col. (USAF Ret.), WWII tow pilot in the 314th TCG, 32nd TCS. Interview by the author, July 1989, Abilene, Tex.

48 Pilot Training Manual, 5.

> double tow the number of gliders were greatly increased and troop carrier ran out of glider pilots for copilots duty. The fighter guy with me John Mesch damn near died of fright.[49]

The power pilots' comments in the reports upon returning from the missions serve to highlight their feelings on the matter.

> As a power pilot I believe that we should be given ground training if we are ever to go in as glider pilots again.[50]

> A pilot (power) who had never been in a glider till DDay. First ride actual combat mission. No knowledge of glider operation and no knowledge of personal protection upon landing. Many men were given weapons for use, which they had never handled before. No instructions given as to use or effectiveness. Glider pilot handicapped by having to instruct power pilot as to flight and protective measures. . . . As a power pilot I believe we should have some training on gliders before going in and some infantry training.[51]

> I'm a power pilot; send men in who have been trained as glider pilots -- not power pilots who have had no infantry training or glider training.[52]

> Power pilots should have ground training before training as glider pilots, such as firing guns, concealment and cooperation,

---

49 F/O James L. Larkin Memorabilia, provided by his son Michael Larkin to the author May 23, 2023.
50 Lt. B. B. Barber and Lt. John L. Wesesky, 437th TCG, "TCMICS - GP," Varsity, GP Interrogation, Serial A 8-9, GP's Attached and Assigned to the 85th TCS, RG 18 Entry #7, Federal Records Center, Suitland, Md.
51 Lt. John A. Miller flying copilot for F/O O. J. Welch, 437th TCG, "TCMICS-GP." RG 18 Entry #7, Federal Records Center, Suitland, Md.
52 Lt. M. M. Meyer and Lt. D. F. Donovan, 437th TCG, "TCMICS -GP," RG 18 Entry #7, Federal Records Center, Suitland, Md.

with airborne... Should be briefed with Airborne so we would know what to do on the ground and what the objectives are and tactics.... I felt very helpless at not being able to navigate or communicate with anyone.... The noise was deafening and several bursts of A/A rocked the glider appreciably after we cut loose, nor could I positively identify any landmarks. We made a wide circuit to the left and finally chose a field to the left (North) of an apparently dry canal (the autobahn) which had fences in it crossing out path and also two wells of the wooden bucket variety. We hit some of the fences, but to help from hitting the trees at the end of the area, we kept turning left and knocked the left wheel off on a crossing road, and skidded sideways to an abrupt stop, the left wing tearing off. The boys went out shooting to into the woods to the west and also into a small clump to our west. I was the last man out and on advice from Lt. Madden left my pack in the glider...[53]

As the saying goes, "There's no atheist in a foxhole," even though I had never been on the frontlines before, it doesn't take one long to learn. I wasn't on enemy soil as much as I was in it![54]

Equally forthright on the subject were the glider pilots,

Copilot was power pilot and had never been in a glider before or had never experienced infantry training! until then![55]

Combat training for throttle jockey copilots.[56]

---

53   Lt. Howard B. Westley, 437th TCG, "TCMICS-GP," RG18 Entry #7, Federal Records Center, Suitland, Md.
54   Lt. K. P. Johnson and Lt. S. H. Merritt, 437th TCG, "TCMICS-GP," RG18 Entry #7, Federal Records Center, Suitland, Md.
55   Lt. K. P. Johnson and Lt. S. H. Merritt, "TCMICS-GP," RG 18 Entry #7, Federal Records Center, Suitland, Md.
56   F/O Harry D. Bradley, "TCMICS-GP," RG18 Entry #7, Federal Records Center, Suitland, Md.

Standing in stark contrast to the glider pilots in the ETO, the combat training for the 1st Air Commandos glider pilots destined for the CBI was unique. While in glider training at Bowman Field, a call for glider pilot volunteers for a secret mission went out. The final group of the 100 chosen received an intense six-week combat training in jungle warfare. This small group of glider pilots were fully prepared for the hostile jungle territory and the enemy they would encounter. Their training consisted of twenty-five-mile marches carrying full gear, hand-to-hand combat and weapons qualifications, and night flying operations, formations, and snatches.[57] The organization of the glider pilots within "Project 9," later called the 1st Air Commandos, was very different from those in the ETO. The commandos were led by two distinguished fighter pilots, Lt. Col. Phillip Cochran and Lt. Col. John Alison, who worked with the other Allied powers to resolve the Burma problem and did not regard the glider pilots or their duties as any different than the other pilots and members of Project 9.

RANK

In an effort to attract volunteers to the glider program, the Army Air Forces offered incentives of rank and rapid advancement. Initially, the men entered at their present grade or, if civilians, as privates. Upon graduation, they were promoted to staff sergeants. Later, the men were admitted to training as staff sergeants, and additional opportunities for officers' commissions were announced. Eventually, all glider pilots were promoted to flight officers, and although the vast majority remained at this rank for the duration of the war, a few received officers' appointments.

Prior to World War II, glider pilots were nonexistent. All military pilots were power pilots, and commissioned officers had to be at least

---

57 Michael H. Manion, *Gliders of World War II: The Bastards No One Wanted*, (Pickle Partners Publishing 2104), 50.

twenty-one years of age with a minimum of two years of college.⁵⁸ When the need for additional pilots in the Army Air Corps began to build and the Glider Pilot Program was introduced, it was realized that the prewar standards could not be applied to attract the needed numbers. In order to preserve its officers' ranks, the Air Corps trained enlisted men who held a high school diploma and graduated them as sergeant pilots. Not only would this preserve the quality of the officers' Corps after the war, but it placed the pilots at a high enough rank to command the planes they flew.

On July 8, 1942, the president signed Public Law 658, creating the rank of flight officer; in essence, it was "a grade above the enlisted ranks but below that of a Second Lieutenant."⁵⁹ The glider pilots referred to it as "the order of the blue pickle" because, as opposed to Second Lieutenants bars, which were blue and rectangular, the flight officers bars were blue and oval on the ends, resembling the shape of a pickle, with a gold bar traversing the center of it horizontally. In actuality, flight officers were the equivalent of a warrant officer (junior grade, W-1), but it was the desire of headquarters (HQ) to see " . . . that these new Flight Officers be accepted in the nature of 'Third Lieutenants' by all personnel and that they be required to comply with, and in turn to be treated in accordance with, all the customs and courtesies of the military service pertaining to commissioned officers."⁶⁰

In another turn of events in June of 1942, despite earlier promises, HQ decided to issue certificates instead of ratings to graduating glider pilots. Those closely involved with the glider program protested, believing the Army Air Corps was breaking faith with the men. In September of 1942, the rating was reestablished, but not before another blow was dealt to the glider pilots' morale.⁶¹

---

58 J. H. MacWilliam and Bruce D. Callander, "The Third Lieutenants," *Air Force Magazine*, March 1990, 100.
59 MacWilliam and. Callander, "The Third Lieutenants", 100.
60 MacWilliam and Callander, "The Third Lieutenants," 100-101.
61 Project Book of the CG, AAFFTC, quoted in Assistant Chief of Air Staff, "AAF Historical Studies: No. 1," 29.

Soon after this incident, the earliest volunteers in the program were graduating. They were required to purchase their silver pilot wings and have them engraved with a "G" over the center to distinguish them from power pilots ("P") and service pilots ("S").[62] Typical of the program, an order was handed down rescinding their graduation. The men were ordered to remove their wings until their completion of a newly installed Advanced training course.[63] They glumly did as ordered and joined the glider pools to await training and "graduation."

On November 21, 1942, a major change in the glider pilots rank was instituted. An act of Congress formally established that sergeant pilots and glider pilots be promoted to flight officers, and the glider aviation students rank upon graduation was changed in accordance with the act. Aviation students who had transferred in from other branches were also provided for: "Commissioned officers training in grade would continue in that grade upon graduation, while those aviation cadets who had voluntarily relinquished pilot training to enter the glider program would be commissioned second lieutenants." [64]

The rank of flight officer was implemented in all the Air Corps' pilot programs, including the Power Pilot Program, which had lowered its entrance requirements and graduated a large number of sergeant pilots. Despite Army Air Forces assurances of "rapid advancement," the rank of flight officer was considered by many of the glider pilots to be a terminal rank from which promotion was impossible, and it was the highest rank the majority of glider pilots ever wore. This only added to the series of letdowns by the Army Air Forces.

Considering the structure of the Troop Carrier Squadron, prospects of promotion were dismal. Organizational charts provided slots for one first lieutenant, one second lieutenant, and twenty-

---

62   It has been long held by the glider pilots, both during and after the war, that the "G" engraved on their wings stands for "GUTS" - a fact few would doubt.
63   Mousseau, interview, 20 June 1989.
64   Daily Diary, AAFFTC, Jan. 2, 1943, quoted in Assistant Chief of Air Staff, "AAF Historical Studies: No. 1," 46.

seven flight officers.⁶⁵ Only two additional positions in the TCG were open to glider pilots. One opening was for a captain in TCG HQ and one for a major in general HQ.⁶⁶ To remedy the sagging morale and disillusionment of the pilots following training delays, inadequate housing conditions, and doubtful promotions, additional measures were taken to fit them into staff and administrative officers' positions in TCC HQ.⁶⁷ The rank of flight officer precluded their ability to do administrative duties.

The glider pilots rank was of primary importance, not only because of the pay and benefits received, but it decided the issue of command. The absence of promotions affected the outcome of many issues facing them in combat. In matters pertaining to the plane they flew, the glider pilots were technically in command even if outranked by an airborne infantry commander. If the pilot was the highest-ranking officer aboard the glider, he was in command until the airborne infantrymen met up with their outfits and commanders, although this was not always the reality in the heat of war. Not all missions and flights went smoothly; therefore, it was imperative that the command structure be clear and meet all contingencies. In the Invasion of Normandy, Flight Officer William Kostiak's flight began with a perfect tow until they were in the overcast and separated from their tow ship. They did not make their LZ and found themselves alone in enemy territory. In the middle of this emergency, the issue of command—who was giving the orders—arose. Flight Officer Kostiak reported,

> ... and the two ship suddenly began to climb and dive into a steep left dive of 900 degrees [90 degrees] that is when the towrope broke. Anticipated Airspeed at this time about

---

65   AFRIT to Air Force Director of Air Support, AC/AS, Program Planning, AS/AS, A-1, Air Force Military Personnel Division, March 17, 1943, in AAG 211, Glider Pilots, quoted in Assistant Chief of Air Staff, "AAF Historical Studies: No. 1," 79.
66   AFRIT to Air Force Director of Air Support quoted in Assistant Chief of Air Staff, "AAF Historical Studies: No. 1," 79.
67   AFRIT to Air Force Director of Air Support quoted in Assistant Chief of Air Staff, "AAF Historical Studies: No. 1," 79.

185 M.P.H. . . . Should get straightened out who is to be in command EM [enlisted men] or glider pilot when forced down alone. GP [glider pilot] should be in com. [command]/ A/B [airborne] E.M. [enlisted men] until reach the LZ. [68]

Captain Baxter also highlighted an additional consequence of a lack of an established command structure:

> . . . lack of coordination between control party and command on dispatching of aircraft.[69]

This issue of who was in command at the time of the glider landing forward was a recurring question that had been clarified by Operation Varsity. This included who was in command until the troops a glider pilot flew in rejoined the airborne they were attached to. The glider pilot would usually be the highest ranking among the occupants of the glider. It was also not uncommon for glider pilots to lead the airborne from their glider into skirmishes to clear the enemy from the field and prevent further casualties. Flight Officer Mahe's Mission Summary Report demonstrates how the glider pilots and airborne worked together when the issue of rank was clear and followed.

> Sgt. Ceszorinski, and myself proceeded S/W, met a French civilian and got our bearings. He also told us that this area was all held by the enemy. We picked up approx. 25 straggler paratroopers, I took charge being of senior rank and we knocked out a MG (machine gun) nest & 6 snipers in the

---

68   F/O James L. Larkin 437th TCG, 96th TCS, "TCMICS-EGPCM," RG18 Entry #7, Federal Records Center, Suitland, Md. F/O Larkin flying with F/O William Kostiak commenting on a corporal who was excited during flight that gave them trouble all fifteen days until they made their way back to their own lines. 437th TCG, 96th TCS., "TCMICS-EGPCM," RG18 Entry #7, 437th TCG, Federal Records Center, Suitland, Md.
69   Captain Baxter O. Simpson, 437 TCG 84 TCS, March 27, 1945, "TCMICS-GP," RG18 Entry #7, Federal Records Center, Suitland, Md.

junction of the roads 1/2-mile N/W of Amfreville. . . . We then proceeded N/E about 2 mi & contacted a large body of paratroopers under Col. Harrison of the 508th. . .[70]

For the glider infantrymen whose first trip into battle was in a glider, the command of the glider pilots was welcome. Flight Officer Harvey Manis commented on the reactions of the airborne during flight and in unloading.

> After landing a little panicky. Settled down when we assumed command.[71]

Flight Officer Manis elaborated in his Interrogation Check Sheet that once the medic reached his glider to tend an airborne soldier hit in the leg ten times during landing, the glider pilots took command of the airborne to unload the glider.[72] For unseasoned airborne troops, especially those arriving on the battlefield for the first time in a glider, possibly airsick and injured, the command of veteran glider pilots may well have provided some reassurances in a confused environment. However, the issue of rank and command was never formally addressed by the AAF. Even though they were usually left to their own devices, the issue of rank and command among the glider pilots seems to have been rarely disputed. With the exception of the 1st Air Commandos, the rank of flight officer, although a promotion, often placed the glider pilots in a precarious position. The rank was new and did not belong to either the enlisted or the officers' ranks. The fact that a flight officer with one year's service outranked an enlisted man with fifteen years did not sit well with some veterans. In effect, the glider pilots were not "third lieutenants," but instead,

---

70   F/O J. A. Mahe and F/O D. F. O'Hora, Handwritten Statement, RG 18, Entry #7, Federal Records Center, Suitland, Md.
71   F/O Harvey S. Manis, "TCMICS-GP," RG 18, Entry #7, Varsity, Serial A-8, GP's Attached and Assigned to 84th TCS, Federal Records Center, Suitland, Md.
72   F/O Harvey S. Manis, "TCMICS-GP."

the equivalent of warrant officers.⁷³

To increase their isolation in the earlier stages of the war, glider pilots were not considered real pilots by many of the power pilots because their planes had no engines. The infantry initially did not accept them, even though they landed and fought in enemy territory; upon landing, the two groups separated, with the glider pilots being evacuated in a matter of days. Perhaps most of all, the dereliction of the AAC/AAF to provide combat training to the glider pilots until 1943, even though they knew the problem existed and were knowingly placing the glider pilot in combat situations, isolated them more than any other factors. As a direct result of these factors, the glider pilots were forced into a class of their own, isolated from the power pilots, the infantrymen, and even the other members of their TCG. An often-quoted description of them by a veteran of the 437th TCG serves as a clear description of these aviator/soldiers who found themselves caught in a complex situation:

> They were the most uninhibited individualists in the army. There seemed to be something about flying a glider or being selected for that job that freed a man from the ordinary restraints of army life. Those that wanted to fight, fought like lions. Those who wanted to get back to Brussels, got back there before anyone else. Once their gliders had landed or crashed there was no flying for them to do. After each airborne operation it had been recommended that glider pilots be organized into units trained in infantry tactics and given a job on the ground. They were usually right up front when the need for men was greatest. But they successfully defied all such attempts at organization.⁷⁴

---

73   Warrant officer was terminal grade and a specialty grade, which, shortly after the war and the division of the Army and Air Force, was the rank Army helicopter pilots wore that restricted their duties to their specialty—flying.
74   Frank Guild Jr. *Action of the Tiger: The Saga of the 437th Troop Carrier Group,* (Battery Press, Inc. Uptown Station, Nashville, Tenn., 1980), 85.

One could ask if such a description is any wonder. It could be argued that their being "freed from the ordinary restraints of army life" was a natural consequence of the AAC/AAF inaction and/or inability to remedy a glaring problem of the combat role of the glider pilot and the accompanying power struggles within the Army Air Forces command, which left the glider pilots at loose ends. If that appears as a harsh judgement, one needs only read the statement of the WWII Army Air Forces official military historians:

> Twice within a single generation the country has been forced into a world conflict; in each case the major enemy was the same, but, as the second war opened, no adequate record of the experiences of the first had as yet been provided for either official or public use. . . . Much of what has been written about the Air Services in World War I had been episodic, personalized, apologetic. Authors who popularized the idea of air power were not trained historians: between the wars they wrote of the future; during the recent conflict they had no choice but to draw their conclusions from incomplete evidence. . . . the historian can render 'the most essential service in determining the public policy relating to National Defense.' But they have taken to heart also this warning that historians 'have been inclined to record victories and gloss over the mistakes and wasteful sacrifices' . . . 'it is very important that the true consequences that make our military history should be matter of common knowledge.'[75]

---

75   The Army Air Forces in World War II, *Plans & Early Operations: January 1939 - August 1942*, Vol. I. edited by W. E. Craven & J. L. Cate, (Washington D.C.: Office of Air Force History, 1983), vii - viii. quoting in part from H.S. Toulmin, *Air Services AEF*, 1918 (New York, 1927), Forward, p. v. and *Selected Speeches and Statements of General of the Army George C. Marshall*, ed. Maj. H. DeWeerd (Washington, 1946), 35-39.

CHAPTER 4
TROOP CARRIER

"... in his opinion their presence [glider pilots] in a troop carrier unit is a demoralizing influence; and his recommendation is that glider units be maintained entirely separate from troop carrier units..."

—Special Interview with Troop Carrier Pilot

Following a glider pilot's graduation from the glider program, he was assigned to a Troop Carrier Command. The primary responsibility of the newly formed TCC was the transportation of paratroopers, air landed, and glider troops and equipment into combat.[1] One TCC was assigned to every theater of war. A TCC consisted of two or more wings, which contained at least two groups; each group was made up of two to four squadrons of 360 men each.[2] Of the 360 men assigned to a squadron, 27 were glider pilots. The remaining number were tow pilots and intelligence, medical, engineering, operations, communications, and transportation personnel. Each squadron was also assigned its own commanding officer (CO), adjutant, plans and training offices, personnel and classification departments, quartermaster, and technical supply.[3] In essence, it was capable of functioning as a separate entity

---

1   Major Kenneth E. Marts, "Troop Carrier Aviation: Its Mission, Organization & Equipment," AAF School of Applied Tactics, AAF Tactical Center, Orlando Fla., Oct. 1944, Microfilm Collection 248.272-8, 2-3, Air Force Historical Research Center, Maxwell AFB, 3.
2   Marts, "Troop Carrier Aviation: Its Mission, Organization & Equipment," 3.
3   Donald L. van Reken, *The 32nd Troop Carrier Squadron: An Airborne C-47 Squadron 1942-1945: Pilots, Paratroops, and Gliders in North Africa, Sicily, England, France and Germany*, (Holland, Mich.: Author, 1989), 1.

within TCC.

The China Burma India Theater was unique in its mission, which required aerial support for the supply of British Major General Orde Wingate. General Wingate was the leader of the 77th Indian Brigade, also known as the Chindits. They waged a form of unconventional warfare in jungle terrain to retake territory from the Japanese and reestablish conventional supply chains. To meet this unusual challenge, the Combat Cargo Command was activated for the purpose of supporting the Allied operations in Burma. The command was very fluid and lacked some of the rigidity and formalization of TCC. This allowed the Combat Cargo Command to act swiftly and with precision in support of the backcountry operations because, in essence, it cut out the red tape. The 1st Air Commando Group's responsibilities included providing aerial cover and supplies for deep in-country penetration missions and evacuation of the wounded. As a result, glider pilots in the 1st Air Commando did not encounter the same issues as those in the ETO.

In cooperation with one another, in the European Theater, the TCG and TCS were responsible for the maintenance of their glider pilots' flying proficiency. Because the extent of preparation considered necessary was subjective, it resulted in a quality and quantity of training between the groups that covered the spectrum. There were several complaints about inadequate flying time, and many glider pilots felt four hours per month was not enough. This could have been caused by back-to-back missions and/or a shortage of gliders or tow pilots or towplanes. While some TCG allowed the glider pilots only minimal flying time, others utilized them in all aspects of operations, including copiloting C-47s, flight training, and administrative work.

Along with the complaints about a lack of flying time between missions, of great concern was the lack of practice flying loaded gliders that handled very differently from empty gliders. Loaded gliders could reduce the glide ratio and cause a glider to stall out. This concern was echoed in a Troop Carrier Aviation: Tactical Doctrine report on Normandy in 1944 that stated that the glider pilots were trained to make "minimum speed landings" with empty gliders. In hindsight, they should have trained with loaded gliders "because the loaded gliders stalled at a higher speed than the empty ones, and the pilots who had been trained in the empty gliders did not realize this."[4] It was recommended from that point forward—training was in loaded gliders. To simulate loaded gliders, practice sandbags would be secured in the cargo area of the gliders.

There were also numerous comments on the glider pilot debriefings about the poor condition of the gliders during missions. This may have been due to a shortage in gliders or the salvage and reuse of gliders, which was accomplished by a method of snatching up the glider by a C-47 in air. This allowed the glider to be removed from the landing zone, if it was salvageable, and undergo repairs, enabling it to be reused in another mission. Normal wear and tear and constant exposure to the weather would have taken a toll on the gliders, as it did on the towropes.

DUTIES

With the 1942 establishment of the new rank of flight officer, which designated a flying specialty, flight officer glider pilots slipped between the administrative cracks when it came to pulling additional duties within their assigned groups and squadrons. Based on his rank, his sole responsibility was to fly. The rank of flight officer did not make the glider pilots fully commissioned officers, despite their title, and therefore, they could not be assigned officers' duties.[5] Those few that were promoted to commissioned officers had additional duties and were often kept very busy. However, when missions were spaced

---

4   Captain Kermit T. Hanson, "Troop Carrier Aviation: Tactical Doctrine," AAF School of Applied Tactics, AAF Tactical Center, Orlando Fla., Nov. 1944, Microfilm Collection 248.272-8, 2-3, Air Force Historical Research Agency, Maxwell AFB, 16.
5   J. MacWilliam and Callander, "The Third Lieutenants," 102.

out and flying time was short, the occupation of the flight officer glider pilots became an issue, as did their pay. Flight officers were paid the same base salary as a junior grade warrant officer ($150 per month), plus an additional $75 in flight pay. Combined, this added up to a little more than the earnings of a second lieutenant stationed overseas.[6] The increased pay for a decreased workload did nothing to soothe the tensions between the glider pilots and other members of the squadrons. Major Frank J. Moore, Commanding Officer of the 51st Troop Carrier Wing Glider Base, described the relationship in a report, recommending glider pilots handle their own administrative work:

> It is my suggestion that this Glider Group be divided in squadrons and be commanded and administered by Glider personnel. My own observations have convinced me of the need for this. When gliders were first used tactically small groups of glider pilots were attached to various troop carrier squadrons, and, frankly, the glider pilots were not treated well. Looked upon, as stepchildren, they did not receive equal consideration with other members of the squadron. As a result, the morale of glider pilots suffered throughout the theater, until Col. Manning, the Commanding Officer of the 51st Troop Carrier Wing, made the decision to organize as a separate glider unit, designated as the 51st Troop Carrier Wing Glider Base. . . . From this time forward . . . morale rose and efficient increased. The glider pilots themselves performed every base function under this set-up. . . . It is essential that the training and briefing for glider operations be conducted and controlled by glider personnel.[7]

---

6 MacWilliam and Callander, "The Third Lieutenants," 102.
7 Air Intelligence Contact Unit (hereafter referred to as AICU), Interview with Major Frank J. Moore, December 18, 1944, Microfilm Collection 142.053T-6, Frame 636, 1, Air Force Historical Research Agency, Maxwell AFB.

Additional statements made by overseas returnees demonstrate the prevalence of such treatment, which was further complicated by the confusion surrounding the flight officer's duties or lack thereof.

> With regard to the employment of glider pilots between missions, this returnee feels that generally their time was more or less completely wasted. He states that a few with initiative and interest were useful in spare time administrative capacities and in the training of enlisted men, but that the large majority of glider pilots did practically nothing. He adds, too, that in his opinion their presence in a troop carrier unit is a demoralizing influence; and his recommendation is that glider units be maintained entirely separate from troop carrier units and that glider pilots be constantly trained in their combat duties instead of spasmodically, as they necessarily are in troop carrier groups.[8]

Another returnee reported,

> There were approximately 15 glider pilots attached to each Squadron of my Group. These men were given some administrative duties, but due to the fact that they were continually shifted, this program did not work out either to the benefit of the Unit or of the individual. The glider pilots were very eager and willing, but their effort lacked organization and direction. The availability of the glider pilots' talent and manpower seems to be forgotten except during periods of preparation for missions.[9]

---

8   AICU, "Special Interview with Troop Carrier Pilot," March 6, 1945, Microfilm Collection 142.053T-6, Air Force Historical Research Agency, Maxwell, AFB.
9   AICU, "Special Interview with Returnee Troop Carrier Personnel (Italy)," May 17, 1945, Microfilm Collection 142.053T-6, Air Force Historical Research Agency, Maxwell AFB.

The spare time of the glider pilots in the ETO between missions became and remained one of the TCG's largest problems throughout the war.

The structure of the 1st Air Commandos in the CBI was less formal, and every man, regardless of rank, chipped in to complete the required work and did their assigned duties. Pilots were responsible for maintaining their own aircraft, and this included glider pilots. If other duties needed to be done, officer and enlisted took part. The glider pilots of the 1st Air Commandos were often busy ferrying gliders, acting as mess officers, or flying as copilots on the transports.[10]

Between missions in the ETO, many glider pilots involved themselves in a variety of activities designed exclusively to kill time. In some cases, they fixed up the officers' and enlisted men's clubs, performed skits, made up drinking songs—which were tributes to themselves—and in general earned their reputation as carousers. They played hard, cocksure that they would be returning from the next mission, though the number of belongings they packed up for those who didn't return belied this. Lt. Col. Paul Mousseau recounted the tradition of the glider pilots he flew with, packing a bottle of liquor in their trunks. If they did not return, their fellow pilots would open the bottle and drink a toast to them. This was not a joyful moment but a way to pay respect to a fallen comrade.[11] On one hand, the loss of one of their own pained them sharply; on the other hand, they had to keep moving on to survive themselves and develop a frame of mind to do so. From his war letters, we can gain a little perspective on how Lt. Paul Mousseau dealt with the mental stresses of war.

> We had a little party the other night, we had been pretty busy working and all the boys were in one piece, nobody lost or killed as of late . . . It's funny how quickly you get used to boy's who go out and don't come back. I always thought if a friend

---

10 2nd Lt. Billy Mohr, "Glider Operations," Air Intelligence Contact Unit, HQ, AAF Redistribution Station No.3, 1st Air Commando Gp Combat Cargo Tank Force 10th Air Force, HQ, AAF Redistribution Station No.3, March 27,1945.
11 Lt. Col. Paul W. Mousseau (USAF ret.) interview with author, 1990.

of mine was killed it would stay on my mind but it didn't, in a couple of days it was forgotten. It's a hell of a way to be but it has to be that way I guess. otherwise the rest of us wouldn't be worth a darn.[12]

The months of inactivity between missions was telling when glider pilots were called on to keep the gliders level in flight over three to four-hour flights, sometimes without the benefit of a copilot. The additional strain on the pilot's arms from the towplane wash, turbulence, overloaded gliders, gliders that had major controls knocked out, and a host of other conditions could be very strenuous. Once landed, they directed and assisted in the unloading of the cargo under enemy fire, marched, crawled, led patrols, stormed houses or machine-gun nests, and engaged in every type of combat. In the end, many thought the prolonged periods of inactivity detrimental to both the men's mental and physical condition. Lt. Mousseau went on to state in his letter how morale was low in his unit at the time, and there was not much to do. He ended by summing the issue up in one sentence.

> "It is better to keep busy since it's not good to give a soldier too much time to think."[13]

What is clear is that, although the issue of rank complicated the issue, the assignment of duties in or out of a combat situation lay with their commanders. The amount and quality of that direction varied from group to group and the theater of operation. Some made full use of the glider pilots while others provided little to no direction for them. Numerous reports from various missions cite issues such as the following:

---

12   Lt. Paul Mousseau to Doris Laferriere, February 11, 1944.
13   Mousseau to Laferriere, February 11, 1944.

> I think there would be far less confusion if each glider pilot remained with his AB unit until the time of evacuation arrived. As it was, the pilots were herded together and a good many of them did not do much. I consider that the leadership of the glider pilots was poor. I did not come in contact with Major Nevins of the 50th Wing, so I am unable to give a first-hand account, but I can report that the glider pilots under his command were greatly confused, but whether this was Major Nevins' fault or not I cannot say.[14]

> From what I saw of the C/P it seemed there was no orderly procedure in handling glider pilots. Many of us would have helped a lot more if the airborne would have sent us to a certain area. For the 1st day and a half, there was no designated area for the glider pilots.[15]

No designated area meant the glider pilots were left to their own devices. It was a fluid situation.

There are also reports of paratroopers not performing duties while in a combat situation and glider pilots picking up their slack. This varied from group to group. Flight Officer Edward Ryan Jr. reported both glider pilots in his glider worked with the airborne sergeant to get it unloaded quickly while the other airborne occupants of the glider refused. Later, they argued with the airborne over evacuating the glider pilots from the command post, when they finally located it.

> Hit power line in dark, uprooted pole and broke lines. Reinforced nose kept pole from coming through. Glider

---

14   Captain Henry Hobbs, 439th TCG 93rd TCS, "Narrative," RG18 Entry #7, Federal Records Center, Suitland Md. In "Recommendations" by Major Nevin's to the upper commands, he was an advocate for the glider pilots in terms of their use, equipment and safety.
15   F/O Martin T. Laffey, 313th TCG, "TCMICS-GP," 313 GP SU, Federal Records Center Suitland Md.

stopped within 30 ft. after the collision. AB got out and spread out on the ground. Sgt. called for them to unload the glider, but they refused. Tisdale [copilot] and Sgt. unloaded the glider. Ryan [pilot] stood guard... Joined by paratroopers. Took up positions along hedgerow but found they were surrounded. Ryan, Tisdale, and half of remaining party crawled out on road and took up new positions. German appeared at opening of culvert and Lt. Tisdale shot him dead. . . . In attempting to locate CP - followed Frenchman who led them to dead paratroopers. . . . gliders crashing upon landing. . .. A/B established hospital and collection point for wounded. Slept that night . . . Next morning stepped out of area to discover the illusive CP only 50 yards away . . . Discovered Lts. Ittner and Levering there injured. Ittner got out of bed, walked out of hospital supported, collecting his glider pilots. Engaged in sniper hunting. 6 collected within 100 yds of CP. Ittner argued with A/B to evacuate the GPs but they insisted the GPs dig in. They determined to make for the beachhead and started for coast to Ste. Mere du Mont. After 1/4-mile Ittner could not go farther and ordered the rest to push on ahead. Ryan and Tisdale hid around the corner and stayed - others went on.[16]

Other glider pilots reported similar issues:

Too many duties performed by glider pilots of this group, while other groups and airborne layed around . . .[17]

Had difficulty with new Airborne troops. Also had trouble evacuating glider.[18]

---

16 F/O Edward A. Ryan Jr. and Lt Paul A. Tisdale, 437th 85th TCS, Handwritten Report, RG 18 Entry#7, Federal Records Center Suitland. Md.
17 F/O Kermit K. Swanson, 437th TCG 84 TCS, "TCMICS-GP," RG18 Entry #7, Federal Records Center, Suitland, Md.
18 2nd Lt. Harold R. [E] Anderson, 437th Group, "TCMICS-GP," 437th Group, Varsity, March 28, 1945, RG18 Entry #7, Federal Records Center, Suitland, Md.

The difficulty with the airborne troops, however, was more the exception than the rule. It reflected not only the command not setting a clear chain of command through objectives and rank and the perpetual struggle between the two commands but also the inconsistencies between Troop Carrier Groups. Most glider pilots had great respect for the airborne troops. They were greatly impressed with their organization, skill, and willingness to help them. The airborne also seemed to willingly accept their help, and many reports reflect the two groups working together for days on end. The glider pilots assured their airborne passengers that they were going to do their best to get them there in one piece, and the airborne troops saved the glider pilots on numerous occasions when the situation was dire. The fact that both pilots and airborne arrived or perished together may have strengthened that bond.

PRE-MISSION TRAINING AND BRIEFINGS

The absence of any pre-mission training and/or conditioning program was often the fault of the mission planners in headquarters; short timetables between glider mission conceptions and D-days also precluded adequate preparation. The invasion of Sicily, the first American glider mission, was a prime example:

> The combat training of glider pilots in this theatre has been inadequate with the exception of the British Glider Pilot Regiment. They were also given an intensive flight training course in the CG-4A glider in this theatre of six weeks duration . . . The plan did not call for the use of American glider pilots in the initial operation so their flight training was neglected, and emphasis was placed on training the British. A change in plans necessitated supplementing with a small number of American glider pilots to go as copilots.[19]

---

19   62nd TCG, "Operation Husky," Mission Reports, 9- 10, RG 18, Entry #7, Federal Records Center, Suitland, Md.

The mission was brutal. American glider pilots copiloted for the British, who had six weeks experience in the American Waco CG-4A. Inexperienced crews of gliders and tows were fired upon by US Naval vessels, and many of the gliders released, or were cut prematurely in the darkness, falling just short of landfall. Paul Gale, a navigator, was concerned that the release coordinates were never changed to take into account the effect of wind in the face of the gliders, especially the forty-five knot gale force winds they encountered that night. The coordinates they had received in the briefings were for five or ten knot winds or calm weather. "If the wind changed then the [release] coordinates had to change."[20] He believes that is why so many gliders ended up in the sea. Many glider pilots and their passengers either drowned under the weight of their own equipment or were illuminated with spotlights and shot as they struggled to stay afloat.

The disaster of Sicily clearly demonstrated the consequences of poor preparation and political jockeying for the use of the airborne by commanders, but to no avail. The situation within the Army Air Forces and TCC continued on its rocky course, and the glider pilots were forced to take what training was made available to them. Unfortunately, in some cases, the problems extended into the quality of some of the pre-mission briefings the glider pilots received.

Subjects routinely covered in pre-mission briefings were the security measures activated, navigational discussions, weather expectations, ground situations to be encountered, and prisoner of war escape and evasion techniques. Their quality, however, depended on the individual squadron's intelligence officer. His responsibilities included the collection and interpretation of the latest enemy information gleaned from reports and photographs. For example, aerial views taken by P-38s up to two hours prior to mission time

---

20 "Operation Ladbroke, Second World War Experience Center," Excerpt of interview by Paul Little 2003 of Paul Gale, C-47 Navigator, https://war-experience.org/events/operation-ladbroke/. Paul Gale completed 64 combat missions before the end of the war.

could prove invaluable in discerning enemy placements in the field where the gliders were to land. Imperative as this information was to the safe transport and delivery of the cargo and glider occupants, it was not always passed on to the glider pilots. The most glaring example of this was in December 1944. While running resupply missions into Bastogne during the Battle of the Bulge, troop carrier pilots, glider and tow alike, were not informed of the cleared corridor through which they could have flown virtually unscathed into the city. Although their TCG had been notified of the 4th Armored Division's breakthrough in ample time to change the flight routes and brief the personnel, nothing was done. As a result, many men died needlessly. Participants in the mission reported,

> Air Corps Major at VIII Corps Hq at Florenville told me that a message had been relayed the previous evening that future resupply missions to Bastogne should follow the corridor opened by 4th Armed Div.[21]

> A Major with the 101st AB Div . . . said, 'Why did you come in that way? You should have approached Bastogne in the manner we suggested by message the evening of 26 December, after the 440th TC Gp had arrived.'[22]

> Lt. Col. Barnes, FA, at Bastogne said that as he saw us flying in he knew we would pass over intense flak, because he had known for some time that the Germans had flak positions on the course we flew. Numerous people with whom I talked at Bastogne seemed to think that we should have known that the corridor had been opened by the 4th Armored Div. At Luxembourg a Lt. Col., AC, connected with G-2 said that

---

21 Lt. Charles R. Brema, Bastogne, 439th TCG 93rd TCS, "TCMICS-GP," RG 18, Entry #7, Federal Records Center, Suitland, Md.
22 Lt. Lloyd G. Clark, Bastogne, 439th TCG 93rd TCS, "TCMICS-GP," RG 18 Entry #7, Federal Records Center, Suitland, Md.

he would like to know who passed out the information that flak was south of the RR, because the fact of the matter was exactly the reverse.[23]

Numerous casualties were incurred in the troop carrier's attempt to get supplies to the encircled 101st Airborne. To make matters worse, following the breakout, Brigadier General Antony McAuliffe of the 101st Airborne replied to an article in *Stars and Stripes* regarding the desperate plight of his men during Bastogne:

> Your Jan. 9 issue carries a photo of the Ninth Troop Carrier Command dropping supplies to us at Bastogne. The caption refers to the "desperate plight of the defenders." To such nonsense I again say "Nuts." Ask those tough cookies of the 101st Airborne, 10th Armored, 705 TD attached artillery and Force Snafu. They really know the score. It was pretty rough at times but we were hurting badly only for medical attention and a little bit for ammunition. Our situation was never desperate and I know of no man inside of Bastogne who ever doubted our ability to hold it.[24]

In fact, the gliders brought in supplies and nine volunteer medical personnel to treat the wounded. The inference that many members of TCC had given their lives in vain sparked heated controversy and dealt another huge blow to the glider pilots' morale. Col. Charles A. Young made this clear in his letter to the commanding general, IX TCC:

> The plain inference from the General's statement is that the Troop Carrier missions were unnecessary. . . .. a not

---

23 2nd Lt. Mack Striplin, Bastogne, 429th TCG 93rd TCS, "TCMICS-GP," RG 18 Entry #7, Federal Records Center, Suitland, Md.

24 Brig. Gen. A. C. McAuliffe, quoted by Col. Charles H. Young in a Memo to commanding general, IX TCC, Jan. 15, 1945, Mission Bastogne, Mission Reports, Federal Records Center, Suitland, Md.

inconsiderable number of lives and aircraft were lost on this mission—fourteen (14) towplanes and as many gliders were shot down out of fifty (50) -- which involved a higher percentage of loss than any other, or in the total of all other missions flown by this group to date, including D-Day in Normandy. . . . We were told that we must get ammunition and medical supplies to the Bastogne pocket or the 101st could not survive. A great many of my men died in that task. Many more are missing in action or prisoners of war. They made the sacrifice gladly, anxious to do anything to help the gallant fighters whom we had taken into Normandy on "D" Day.

What am I to give as an answer now to those of my men who survived the terrible flak and machine gun fire and to the families of those who did not, when they ask why they were sent in on a task which the General now, in effect, says was not necessary? The word "Nuts" does not seem appropriate.[25]

Not only did the actions of the men who voluntarily risked their lives go unappreciated, but many of them lost their lives because of the incorrect information passed out in the briefings. In the China Burma India Theater, it was only due to last-minute photographs ordered before Operation THURSDAY by Colonel Phillip Cochran on a hunch—and against orders which discovered literally minutes prior to takeoff—that one of the landing sites, Piccadilly, was covered with teak logs that would have surely resulted in the deaths of many of the glider pilots and the troops they carried if they landed there. General Wingate had forbidden any pre-mission photos of the landing sites for fear of alerting the Japanese of their upcoming movements. By defying these orders, Colonel Cochran saved many of his glider pilots' lives.

Similar incidents occurred when glider pilots were briefed separately from power pilots and received a shorter rendition of

---

25   McAuliffe, Memo Col. Charles H. Young in a Memo to commanding general 1-2.

the mission, objectives, and additional pertinent information. Numerous glider pilot reports stated a request to be briefed with the tow pilots rather than a separate briefing. However, the majority of their complaints were aimed more at the quality of the aids and maps used, as opposed to the subject matter. Almost always, the total absence of visual aids was cited as a problem:

> Better visual aids should be had. Airborne should have better security before missions.[26]

> Photos not very good and maps inadequate.[27]

> Insufficient time for briefing. Briefed D - 3 desired. Smaller groups for briefing. Insufficient maps.[28]

> We believe that the photomap provided at briefing was inadequate since it did not show terrain features clearly. We think this criticism applies to all A/B Missions flown in the E.T.O.[29]

> Sizes of fields quoted - untrue - 200 yds - actually appx 50 yds.[30]

Given the high numbers of poor-quality ratings particular TCG received in both the first and last mission reports, it can be assumed that their briefing techniques and aids did not improve with time.

---

26   Lt. Oddis D.[T] Carroll and Lt. Dennis J. McLaughlin, 437th TCG 85th TSC, "TCMICS-GP," Varsity Serial A-8, GP's Assigned and Attached to 83rd TCS, RG 18 Entry #7, Federal Records Center, Suitland, Md.
27   Lt. Robert E. Neumeister and F/O Charles J. Levendoski, 437th TCG 85th TSC, "TCMICS-GP," RG 18 Entry #7, Federal Records Center, Suitland Md.
28   Major Willis J. Evans, 437th TCG, "TCMICS-GP," RG 18 Entry #7, Federal Records Center, Suitland, Md.
29   F/O Robert C. Moore and F/O James O. Renwick, 439th TCG 95th TCS "TCMICS-GP," RG 18 Entry #7, Federal Records Center, Suitland, Md.
30   F/O Charles W. Dorney Jr., 313th TCG 47th TCS, "TCMICS-GP," 313 GP S11, Microfilm Collection, 249. Air Force Historical Research Agency, Maxwell, AFB.

It also did nothing to increase the already dismal chance of a glider pilot's survival; sometimes the incorrect or sketchy information placed him at a higher risk.

Terrain features revealed in reconnaissance photographs were imperative for the glider pilots to locate their landing zones. They revealed features they used to guide themselves and obstacles to be avoided as they were gliding toward their landing zones. The possible careless interpretation of this information by intelligence officers led to many unnecessary casualties. The Invasion of Normandy was one such situation. Many of the pilots had been informed that the hedgerows surrounding the landing zones were low bushes that could be flown through; in actuality, they were dirt embankments topped with fifty-foot trees. Gliders were ripped apart, and men fell to their deaths when pilots came in for a low-approach landing, unable to clear the tops of the trees because they did not have any means to power the glider to gain enough altitude.

EVACUATION

The immediate reporting to the command post and return of the glider pilots to their home bases to fly additional missions was considered top priority, regardless of the ground action. In the review of Operation Market, it was stated,

> Designated glider and airborne personnel should take immediate charge and issue directions to incoming glider pilots as to the changeable location of the C.P.[31]

In the face of the dynamic situation on the ground, combined with a lack of maps and unpredictable combat situations facing the glider pilots, they were issued standing orders:

---

31 Intelligence Report, Reporting Procedure, 313th TCG, RG 18 Entry 7, Market, September 1944. 63.

The exigencies of the existing situation may preclude evacuation by air to the appropriate home stations, and under the circumstances, glider pilot[s] will be expected to use their own ingenuity to effect their return to the organization to which they were attached for the operation.[32]

As a consequence of following such orders, glider pilots were rumored to depart from battle areas to "wander" around at leisure. This has become one of the greatest fallacies affecting the glider pilots' reported behavior in combat. In his memo, Col. Manning stressed "to which they were attached." Undoubtedly the men traveling singularly or in pairs, hitching rides in jeeps and airplanes, could have shortened their routes home by avoiding places such as Paris and shortening the time they spent there. However, there is a wide discrepancy between their rumored actions and their standing orders.

Perhaps the movements of individual soldiers were misconstrued since large-scale evacuations were the preferred method of moving glider pilots out. Regardless, the fact remains that any unauthorized absence from the combat area would have clearly been a case of desertion; yet, in over 700 reports researched, only one such case was discussed, which included five glider pilots and a court martial recommended, but there was no evidence this court martial took place. In that case, the five glider pilots returned after D+2 with the help of the Dutch underground; however, glider pilots were ordered to return to their CP or home bases by any means necessary as soon as possible. The reason stated for the court martial recommendation was this: "Every man with a gun was needed by the 82nd A/B."[33] This goes against all mission evacuation orders for the glider pilots unless specific orders were given. Many times, just the opposite took place,

---

32 Lt. Col. Robert B. Cox, Acting Adjutant General, Memo to Commanding Officer 62nd TCG, 64th TCG, Evacuation of Glider Pilots, August 13, 1944, RG 18 Entry #7, Federal Records Center, Suitland, Md.
33 Col. H. Nevins to Colonel G.M. Jones, "Recommendations," Headquarters 50th TCW, October 1, 1944. Air Force Historical Research Agency, Maxwell AFB.

and the glider pilots threw in with the airborne, against standard procedure, and were criticized for not returning sooner.[34] Either planned or unplanned, the glider pilots' evacuation was a necessity, for they were not equipped to remain behind enemy lines for more than a two- to three-day stretch. Their limited rations and ammunition became an issue when evacuation took longer periods of time.

In accordance with Air Force directives, the pilots were to report to the division CP after landing and unloading, where they were to remain until released by the commanding officer. Many times, however, the CP had been moved due to some unforeseen difficulty. The glider pilots were not briefed as to the new location and, many times, were unable to locate it. Instead, they joined the airborne forces for a few days or until the area was cleared or made their way back to base. If and when they did reach the CP, the glider pilots were assigned duties such as acting as runners, guarding prisoners, perimeter defense, and supply pickups.[35] A large percentage of the pilots also volunteered for more hazardous duties, including fighting with the airborne infantry and going on enemy patrol. By and large, patrols were a necessary evil; intelligence had to be gleaned about the actual whereabouts of the enemy, his strength, and his intentions. Even if the glider pilot patrols could not assess the situation, they were usually required to bring back prisoners who might, wittingly or unwittingly, divulge some useful information. Being of the opinion that great numbers of glider pilots remained completely unoccupied in a war zone, in August of 1944, one month prior to Operation Market, Major J. Nevins recommended to the commanding general of IX TCC:

> Some constructive use be made of the great numbers of

---

34 In one case, it was learned that the missing glider pilots had not taken a leisurely tour back to their home base but had instead been fighting with the armored tanks for weeks.

35 Supply pickups consisted of rounding up A/B supplies dropped *in* the area (enemy territory). The patrols and their purposes can best be described by John Ellis in *The Sharp End: The Fighting Man in World War II* (New York: Charles Scribner's Sons, 1980).

glider pilots required to remain in Division CP area. 90 PW [prisoner of war] guards and 50 reserve perimeter guards were employed. The remaining 400 odd glider pilots were confined in the CP area literally stewing in their own juice for 3 days with pitched battles going on less than five (5) miles away. It was impossible to prevent some glider pilots from leaving the CP area in search of action against the enemy.[36]

Glider pilots were able-bodied servicemen, and in critical times of need, all servicemen were expected to fight. In Operation MARKET GARDEN—the same mission Gavin said the glider pilots were ill-equipped and ill-prepared for—Gavin needed men on the lines. The glider pilots were military members, on the ground, behind enemy lines, and sent to fill a critical need at the time. However, they were sent without rations, bedrolls, or water for up to seven days. As recorded in Flight Officer William Wescoat's interrogation report, the glider pilots of the 61st and 313th groups were told to leave everything, including their equipment, behind and take only their weapons, ammunition, and entrenching tools.

> [D+3] 23:30 Maj Nevins, 50th Wing - moved all the GPs of the 61st & 313th GPs to the front lines against the Reich Wald. Maj Nevins said guard would be left on our equipment. We were told to just take weapons, ammunition & entrenching tools & to leave everything else in our fox holes. we marched to the front lines and dug in - F/O's Lothringer, Thrash, Schumacker, Avignone, Wescoat reported to the 505th AB for duty. Dig foxholes & established guards - 88's, mortars & small arms fire all night. . . . D+6 we went to B.V area at Mook Station to pick up equipment left there - every thing

---

36   Major J. Nevins, Recommendations to commanding general IX TCC, Aug. 21, 1944, Microfilm Collection, 546.452K, Frame 230, Air Force Historical Research Agency, Maxwell AFB.

had been stolen ... had not supplied adequate guards for our equipment. We were relieved at the front by GPs from the 50th Wing ... [37]

Is it possible that, because of orders like this, the glider pilots arrived without the majority of equipment that reports such as General Gavin's written after Market, highly critical of the glider pilots' preparation and lack of equipment resulted?[38]

Flight Officer Wescoat's report is confirmed in its accuracy by the findings in an official report compiled after Market. The glider pilots under Major Nevins were ordered to leave their equipment, move to the front lines, and remain two to a foxhole. One firearm was issued between the two men. The reasoning was that one could sleep while the other was on watch.[39] Three hundred glider pilots moved up to the front lines, with presumably 150 weapons. It is not clear what happened to the weapons. Repeated German attacks took place during the seven days and nights they were on the front line. When the glider pilots returned to retrieve the equipment they were ordered to leave behind, ten hours later than expected, they found it was all gone. The Airborne Flight Artillery troops had moved through in their absence.

The glider pilots were then ordered back up to the front again.[40] After spending another night on the front, they were evacuated the following morning. They were placed on an evacuation truck intended for paratroopers going into the action, not glider pilots moving out of it. When this was discovered, they were driven about a dozen miles, dropped in the woods, and told to remain concealed. Another truck finally arrived to transport them to Brussels for

---

37 F/O William L. Wescoat 61st TCG 59th TCS, Operation Market, Microfilm 61st TCG HI/SU, Air Force Historical Research Agency, Maxwell AFB.
38 See Gavin's remarks on page 44.
39 "Ground Activities of Glider Pilots," Market, September 1944, 313th TCG, RG18 Entry #7, 17.
40 "Ground Activities of Glider Pilots," Market 17.

evacuation. This convoy was ambushed by the Germans and the road cut off. The glider pilots were under constant fire, in ditches for hours, and finally, under this barrage, they unhooked the trailers from the trucks and slowly inched the trucks back out of the range of fire. They saved fourteen of seventeen vehicles.[41]

That glider pilots ended up engaged in combat either through orders or on their own initiative is clear. It is also clear that their engagement in combat was by no means an isolated incident or due to exigent circumstances. Perhaps Lt. John Coe's report after Operation Market epitomized the glider pilots' opinion on the matter:

> The next day we somehow got tied up with the 506th Paratroopers and went north with them. Having been told at the CP that the glider pilots could not be evacuated for at least two more days, we felt we were doing more good with some infantry outfit, doing what we could, than sitting in a woods doing nothing. And every unit I was with was more than glad to have us.[42]

Despite numerous requests that the AAF tried to resolve the problem, no action was taken. Some glider pilots were resigned to the matter:

> Still the same old story of being evacuated - I doubt if any preparation had been made toward evacuation.[43]

> The process of evacuation of glider pilots is very poor.[44]

> Evacuated on my own from the C.P because I was left behind.

---

41 "Ground Activities of Glider Pilots," Market 17.
42 Lt. John W. Coe, "TCMICS-GP," RG18 Entry #7, Federal Records Center, Suitland, Md.
43 F/O Donald O'Hora, 437th TCG 85th TCS, "TCMICS-GP," RG18 Entry #7, Federal Records Center, Suitland, Md.
44 F/O Donald O'Hora, 437th TCG 85th TCS, "TCMICS-GP," RG18 Entry #7, Federal Records Center, Suitland, Md.

> ... Met the 50th Wing learning that we couldn't go because evacuation ship wasn't assigned to us. We walked back to our C.P. and ran into sniper fire along the way... Went to find the first aid station and had the blisters painted on my feet. The group was gone when I returned. An enlisted man told me they were evacuated. I went to Major Evans and had my evacuation slip signed. He told me to leave with another group. Their captain was there but he started his men before I could catch up. The captain caught up with his men on a motorcycle. I finally caught up with a combination of 435th and 436th men and followed them. My feet were badly blistered and I fell behind after we were ferried across the river Rhine. About five (5) of us got to a wrecked town and stayed in a wrecked house. About late evening I found some of the other fellows who were leaving Monday morning and rode to them to B-66.[45]

Perhaps Flight Officer McDonough summarized it best:

> We did all jobs around the CP until Tuesday morning when we marched down the road to be evacuated only to return to the CP since the evacuation proceedings were "snafu" as usual. Back at CP I was taken in hand by an Airborne Major for the 502 parachute infantry to serve as a runner.[46]

Flight Officer McDonough's evacuation can explain his frustration. He found himself engaged in multiple skirmishes and cut off by Germans. He hitched a ride with another GP, and they were cut off again and sent on a reconnaissance patrol with three other airborne. He eventually managed to hitch a ride on a supply truck headed to Brussels and, from there, made his way back to home base.

---

45 2nd Lt. Glenn W. Danks, Detached Service, 437thTCG 74th TCS, "TCMICS-GP," RG18 Entry #7, Federal Records Center, Suitland, Md.
46 F/O John McDonough, 437th TCG 83rd TCS, "TCMICS-GP," RG18 Entry #7, Federal Records Center, Suitland, Md.

For those out conducting voluntary or assigned duties, the glider pilots could find their evacuation transportation had gone without them and in a few instances had taken their bags. Like McDonough, they were then forced to find their own way back to their home base. Even if they were part of the evacuation, the evacuations were sometimes bottlenecked or delayed, leaving the glider pilots in a city, trying to locate a place to stay, while they waited for the bottleneck to clear. Although there may have been glider pilots that did take off for the large cities for a self-imposed R&R, this does not appear to be the norm. In fact, unless they were issued escape and evasion kits, chances are they would not have any foreign currency to spend for days on end in the cities.

It is entirely possible that a glider pilot in enemy territory, without extensive combat training, maps, or a compass, possibly having suffered from a blow to the head or a serious head injury upon landing, trying to locate a CP in active enemy territory, would be wandering into units and then back out in his quest for protection and to locate where he was and where he needed to go. Additionally, groups of young men who may have just witnessed the injury and deaths of other soldiers and friends, full of adrenalin themselves, would likely be discontent sitting for days while combat raged close by. It should be noted that the glider pilot command reiterated often that the glider pilots must report immediately to their CP upon landing or make their way back to their home bases as soon as possible, and at one point, they threatened to withhold pay. In some cases, when glider pilots failed to return after a reasonable time, they were listed as missing in action.

EQUIPMENT

Prior to a mission, security measures were increased: both incoming and outgoing mail was held, phone calls were forbidden, and all briefed personnel were held under armed guard behind barbed wire until escorted to the field for takeoff. Meals were served within the enclosed area, and men were escorted to the latrines to ensure that there were no outside contacts. To further enhance security, combat equipment was issued just prior to mission time. In theory, this would prevent landing locations from being pieced together by the type of equipment being carried.

Both the gliders and pilots were equipped on combat missions. For overwater flights, a five or seven-man inflatable rubber dinghy was usually stored behind the cockpit; it also served as a ballast, keeping the nose of the glider down when unevenly loaded.[47] Even though the raft contained all the necessary equipment for survival, it was rarely used because of the glider's ability to float for short periods of time.[48] It was also probably left behind in the rush to escape a ditched glider. In his ditching report, Flight Officer Benson Reed described this incident:

> The glider was then brought down on the water at a speed of fifty miles an hour. Upon landing in the water the tail of the glider hit the water several times and a large wave swelled directly into the front of the glider. Fortunately, an air-sea rescue boat was spotted and the glider pilot had been headed in that direction. All the men struggled to get out. The glider pilot broke through the window on the left side, one passenger tore a hole through the top, one went through the emergency door and the others escaped through the back door. All the men were rescued from the water almost immediately and the glider was still afloat as the rescue boat left.[49]

---

47   Lt. Col. Paul W. Mousseau (USAF ret.), interview by the author, 20 June 1989, Fresno, California.
48   In one case, a glider pilot ditched in the Mediterranean, and floated on his glider wing for three days when his tow ship failed to report his location. When asked about this incident, Lt. Col. Mousseau (USAF ret.) stated that although gliders normally didn't float that long, in this instance, it may have been due to the high salt content of the water. Mousseau, interview, 20 June 1989.
49   Lt. Robert Roman Intelligence Officer, "Ditched Glider," 316th TCG RG 18 Entry #7, Federal Records Center, Suitland, Md.

Mae Wests (inflatable flotation vests) were also issued to the men as added protection, but there were complaints of crushed ribs when the devices were worn with heavy equipment.

Two first aid kits were located in the glider, one in the dinghy, and the other, the aeronautics first aid kit, hung on the inside of the glider near the rear door. It had, among its contents, halazone tablets for water purification and two morphine syrettes.[50] Toward the latter part of the war, the morphine syrettes were removed from the kits because of their high theft rate by glider passengers. Each pilot also carried a smaller version of the aeronautical first aid kit on their person.

The glider pilots' clothing and equipment were unique in that they were outfitted as both aviators and infantrymen. As part of their personal aviators' equipment, they were issued flak seat pads, armored vests, and aprons. The flak seat pads were placed on the plywood seats in the cockpit. Few men had faith in the ability of these alone to stop flak; so, prior to a mission, the pilots scrounged any additional scrap metal they could to sit on. If not much metal could be found, they stacked more plywood seats on their own.[51]

Flak vests and aprons were issued as the glider pilots' only protection from metal projectiles. The vests were worn on top of their infantry outfits and attached at the shoulder for quick release on the landing zones. Unlike the vests issued to power pilots, who sat in armored seats, the M-1 vest issued to the glider pilots was

---

50 The aeronautics first aid kit also included three first aid dressings; one tourniquet; one bottle of Halazone tablets; one box of adhesive bandages; one pair of 4" scissors; iodine applicators; two tubes of sulfadiazine (later tablets were substituted), used in the treatment of Meningitis; one box of sulfanilamide, used to treat a variety of infections; an eye dressing unit; and one tube of burn ointment. C.G. Sweeting, *Combat Flying Equipment: U.S. Army Aviators' Personal Equipment, 1917-1945*, with a Foreword by Donald S. Lopez, (Washington D.C.: Smithsonian Institution Press, 1989), 209.

51 Mousseau, interview, 20 June 1989.

armored in both the front and the back.[52] The M-4 apron attached to the glider pilot's vest and covered the lap area.[53] The glider pilots were not, however, issued the groin armor designed to protect the legs. The use of anti-flak garments was relatively new, and it took some time for the AAF to convince aviators that the vests offered more protection if they were worn than if they were placed on the floor under the pilots' legs to stop flak from entering the plane.[54]

The combat helmet, issued as part of the pilots' infantry gear, substituted as protective headgear during the flight while the passengers used their own to sit on as armored seating or to vomit in on a rough ride.[55] Loose helmets flying around the plane upon landing could turn into projectiles, causing serious damage to anyone hit by one. Although repeatedly requested, few glider pilots were issued goggles to protect their eyes in case of enemy fire, a broken or released towrope, winds, or other projectiles that shattered or blew out the gliders' plexiglass windscreens. If their eyes weren't injured, the pilots still faced winds up to or exceeding 120 miles per hour, blowing directly into their eyes if the front portion of the plexiglass was knocked out. If that happened, he still needed to fly, avoid other gliders, choose a landing field, and land the glider with winds and possible debris blowing in his face.

---

52   The vest weighed 17 pounds 6 ounces and protected 3.82 square feet. Col. James B. Coates, Jr. and Major James C. Beyer (eds.), "Wound Ballistics" (Washington, D.C.: Office of Surgeon General, Department of the Army, 1962), p. 672, quoted in Sweeting, *Combat Equipment*, 128.
53   The M-4 Apron weighed 7 pounds, 2 ounces and covered 1.66 square feet, Sweeting, *Combat Equipment*, 129.
54   Sweeting, *Combat Equipment*, 131.
55   The chin strap was often not worn in either in flight or in combat. Those combat tried were aware the concussion from a nearby explosion would cause the helmet to be pulled off, and the chin strap would either break the wearer's neck or actually sever the head from the neck.

In Wesel, Germany, following the last mission of the war in the European Theater of Operations, glider pilots in combat gear are standing near a foxhole trench on the edge of an open field. Operation Varsity was one of the deadliest missions for glider pilots. The Germans dug in and waited for the gliders to get close to the ground before firing. The glider pilots have much more gear than earlier photos shown. There appears to be a khaki uniform shirt on the glider pilot on the left, F/O Harry Friday 435th TCG, 78th TCS. He is carrying three grenades. The glider pilot in the middle is F/O Ed Bilbrey 435th TCG, 78th TCS. The amount of equipment they have strapped to them was one of the main reasons they continually asked for pants with more pockets, which were never supplied. The glider pilot on the right, F/O Eldon Johnson 435th TCG, 78th TCS, has two items that were often requested—goggles and what looks to be a sleeping bag (versus a blanket, which was normally issued and the glider pilots found cumbersome). Photo courtesy of Silent Wings Museum.

Parachutes, which were issued to the glider pilots on routine, noncombat flights, were locked up on combat missions. Army Air Forces reasoning behind this was unclear. However, because parachutes were not issued to the glider infantry, it would have been fruitless to issue them to the pilots. Lt. Col. Paul Mousseau explains,

> We could not have used the parachutes in any case. The exit was through the very back and both the pilot and copilot would have had to run past up to thirteen fully equipped infantrymen without parachutes to get out. There was not much chance of that happening.[56]

There were numerous eyewitness accounts of men falling to their deaths when gliders lost parts of their fuselage, causing the contents to spill out when shot by anti-aircraft guns in flight. In many of these cases, parachutes could have prevented the unnecessary loss of lives of glider pilots and their glider infantry.

The glider pilots' uniforms were another odd combination of aviator/infantry clothing. The AAF required aviators to wear their service uniforms underneath their flight suits to prevent downed pilots from being picked up as spies. The glider pilots, however, were not issued flight suits; during the winter months, they wore their infantry clothing on top of their service uniform, most commonly their khakis, for warmth. In the summer months and in warmer climates, they discarded their service uniform and simply wore their infantry uniforms with their glider wings pinned to the inside of their breast pocket flap. The placement of the wings prevented their being used as a shiny target by the enemy, but if captured, the pilot could lift the flap and prove he was an Army Air Force pilot. More importantly, it also ensured their being assigned to a Luftwaffe POW camp if any were nearby, guaranteeing better treatment than in the Wehrmacht camps.[57]

---

56   Mousseau, interview, 20 June 1989.
57   Mousseau, interview, 20 June 1989.

During the first few combat missions, there was no combat uniform, infantry or otherwise, for the glider pilots. Instead, they wore their khaki service uniforms into battle, usually with their service shoes since combat boots were not issued to them until much later. When the infantry uniforms were assigned, they were strongly disliked, mainly because they lacked pocket space. Following every mission, jumpsuits similar to those worn by the paratroopers were requested. All the jumpsuit's pocket space would have replaced much of the clothing and packs, which made up the infantry uniform and reduced the bulk. It was actually fortunate they were not issued the paratroopers boots, as the Germans in some invasions were ordered to shoot paratroopers on sight. They identified them by their jump boots.

As flight or commissioned officers, glider pilots were issued a musette bag for their extra items. They were also issued a standard infantry field bag in which they were supposed to carry a raincoat, a towel, a bottle of Halazone tablets, a tin of insecticide powder, two heating units, two "K" and one "D" rations, and their mess kit. Additional items carried in the bags were gas masks, eye shields, tubes of protective ointment (1), and tubes of eye ointment (1).[58] During flight, the bags were stored behind the pilots' seats, where they could be grabbed on the way out. In some cases, the field bag was used to hold any extra ammunition the pilot might carry, the rest of which was hung from a webbed belt and suspenders that held their grenades, a canteen, and an entrenching tool. As a rule, the pilots were issued six Mark II grenades, a trench knife, and a .45 pistol. The .45, supposedly standard equipment for officers, was issued to the glider pilots based on availability. It could be worn in a holster around the hips or in a shoulder holster. On the odd occasions the glider pilots were issued sleeping bags or bedrolls, they were attached to the field packs, which pilots carried on their backs.

---

58 "Operation Bigot Anvil," 62nd TCG, Operational Orders 31-32, RG 18, Entry #7, Federal Records Center, Suitland, Md.

Three unidentified glider pilots dressed combat ready. Notice the differences in dress under their top layers. The glider pilots on the right may be in more of his service uniform with a tie versus the other two glider pilots. Their pants were bloused over their boots but initially not all the glider pilots were issued boots. Paratroopers were issued gaiters, which differentiated them from glider pilots and glider infantry. Also notice the lack of pockets. This was an issue the glider pilots complained about throughout the war. Photo courtesy of the Silent Wings Museum Foundation of the Military Glider Pilots Association.

As further protection, each glider was issued a .45 submachine gun and 100 rounds of ammunition, which was assigned to and carried by the copilot. In addition, a rifle, a semi-automatic or automatic weapon, was assigned. The pilots could be issued any one of the following: a 9 lb., 12 oz., .30 M-1 Garand; a 5.50 lb., .30 M-2 carbine rifle, semi- or fully automatic; a .30 M-1 carbine; a 20 lb. Browning Automatic Rifle, firing either singly or at 500 rpm; a .45, submachine gun M-3 with a folding stock, which enabled it to be shot as a pistol or from the shoulder, more often referred to as the "grease gun," firing 350-450 rpm; or the .45 Thompson submachine gun.[59] The weapon issued was indifferent to any training the men may or may not have had or the terrain for which it was best suited, instead being entirely dependent on availability.[60] Although the pilots were ordered to return the weapons to base with them, more often than not, they turned them over to paratroopers or incoming airborne and infantry who had lost their own. This was all they could do for the infantry, which was in every way better supplied.

The glider pilots' performance in combat was further complicated by the lack of necessary items. In a report reviewing Operation Market, escape kits and aid purse were discussed:

> All units of this Wing were provided with sufficient escape aids for pilots and navigators; however, the glider pilots should be provided with these escape aids as well. It is known that the Airborne were provided with an amount of Dutch currency, while the glider pilots were not thus provided. Groups were instructed to issue Escape purses to glider pilots wherever possible.[61]

These items were essential to operate in enemy territory and help locate posts, but they were rarely issued to the glider pilots. Lt. Col. Mousseau remembers only two missions when they had escape and evasion kits. The kits' contents included a map of the landing area, a tiny compass which could be swallowed and retrieved later, currency for the country, and sometimes a passport with a photo of the pilot in civilian clothes. These were considered a great help by the pilots;

---

59   Howard R. Crouch, *U.S. Small Arms of World War 2: A Guide for the Collector, Shooter, & Historian* (Falls Church, Va.: SCS Publications, 1984), 197-98.
60   In theory, the pilot and copilot were outfitted to operate as a team. One should have always been issued an automatic weapon in order to protect the glider and its cargo.
61   Intelligence Report, Reporting Procedure, 313 TCG, Market, September 1944. RG 18 Entry #7, Federal Records Center, Suitland, Md., 61.

the map enabled them to pinpoint their location after landing and make their way to the CP. In dire circumstances, the pilots were also able to offer money for assistance or food. The review of Operation Market goes on to state:

> Upon interrogation glider pilots advocated that they be equipped with the following combat aids in addition to those aids regularly issued: 1) Invasion money and aid kits 2) Maps leading to the LZ and a detailed map of the LZ. Maps of the route are needed in case of a forced landing before the LZ is reached. Glider pilots should also be given ample time to study the maps before the briefing. 3) A photo of the LZ area for detailed study before the mission. 4) Infantry sleeping bags should be obtained for all glider pilots. Blankets are too unwieldy. 5) Jump pants which have large pockets to carry equipment in, thus eliminating bags. 6) Arms: Glider pilots should be permitted to choose weapons with which they have been given ample opportunity to become proficient. In addition, they should be armed with .45 pistols. Usually, upon evacuation, other firearms are turned over Airborne ground troops.[62]

The consistent issuance of these articles and other tools of war would have undoubtedly made the glider pilots' time behind enemy lines a little easier, put him on the same footing as other American soldiers in theater, and spared them much criticism. Despite the lack of clear mission objectives given, suitable weapons, and/or arms training and requested combat gear, the glider pilots performed courageously in a combat infantry role, one in which they could not avoid and were often unequipped for.

---

62 Intelligence Report, Reporting Procedure, 313th TCG, Market, September 1944, RG 18 Entry #7, Market, September 1944, 63.

CHAPTER 5

COMBAT

"I'll tell you straight out. If you've got to go into combat, don't go by glider. Walk, crawl, parachute, swim, float — anything! But don't go by glider."

—Walter Cronkite reporting as an American War Correspondent[1]

IN COMBAT

The glider pilots' contribution to the war effort was invaluable; however, the quality of their performance in battle has been debated by some. The obscurity surrounding their prescribed role in combat was a direct result of the atmosphere that prevailed in the Army Air Corps concerning the Glider Pilot Program. Originated simply as a means of moving men, vehicles, and weapons behind enemy lines, the glider pilot's involvement in ground action was not prepared for until 1943, two years and two months after the acceptance of the first glider pilot students and three months prior to the first glider mission in Sicily. According to the AAF, his mission to deliver arms and men to a rendezvous point behind enemy lines did not include participation in ground combat with the infantry troops he carried. Yet too often, events on the ground required the glider pilots to engage in hostilities. Even though he was to act singularly as a troop carrier, he proved to be a soldier of determination and courage. Often crash landing, sometimes untrained, ill-equipped, and isolated, he had to become an independent fighting force, joining

---
1 R. Ray Otensie, "Gliders: From Wright Field to the Netherlands."

up with the airborne troops or reaching the CP and defending it, guarding or transporting prisoners, acting as a runner, moving to the front lines, or any number of other potentially dangerous jobs.

Despite their perception of their expendability in the eyes of the Army Air Forces, the glider pilots did not shrink back but continued to volunteer for missions such as Bastogne. Eventually, the combat experiences of veteran glider pilots, combined with the technical knowledge of the Troop Carrier Command combat course graduates, created a highly effective and efficient fighting force. Regardless of the commands efforts to focus more on the glider pilot's needs, the glider pilots still remained the poor relations of the power pilot program, their requests often the lowest priority when it came to equipment. Despite this handicap, they performed well. After the Invasion of Normandy, Flight Officer W.V. Stahlman, copilot, filed the Glider Pilot interrogation check sheet for his pilot, Flight Officer J. L. Zumwalt, who was still missing at the time.

> Landed at 3 (30.7) - (98.2) with 3 other gliders in same field . . . There were German M/G [machine guns] on two sides of us. We were strafed in the air & on the ground. . . Dispersed & then hid around that area all morning. Went to R.R. bridge over Merderet in morning and had to wade through water up to our shoulders to get there. Met with the 507th A/B. Coming down tracks towards their regimental C.P. . . . The 507th were to take Granville but it was to hot for them. Snipers got four of the A/B on the way down. At C.P. we went on guard duty GP Smith & I were relieved & went back to C.P. I went to 82nd C.P. about 1600 on D Day. Dug in at 82nd C.P. There I met A/B. We went out on patrols til 2100 & got back in our holes. I guarded the area. Turned in all but two clips as the A/B needed the ammunition. Watched Horsas come in they were being strafed and had poor fields to get into. We circled some snipers in LZ

'O.' I drew fire so that A/B could get him and they did.[2]

Flight Officer J.A. Mahe recounted his actions in Normandy:

> The Col. had us deploy along the road thru La Persquerie and we had very active engagements with the enemy. I used hand grenades & a Browning Auto rifle that I had picked up. In several instances I caught the German hand grenades before they exploded and tossed them back. At night we retired to a field n/o [north of] town & dug in. We moved about 0200 under cover of darkness just prior to a mortar barrage being laid in the field. We worked out was s/w to the 507 C.P. approx 1/2 mile w/o [west of] Amfreville arriving there at dawn. We dug in here with the 507th and resisted a strong German force for the entire day up to about 2300. We then heard the bombardment of the coast, tho't that the 1st Army was coming in and withdrew to the East, infiltering thru German lines attempting to join them. . . . Paratroopers reported they had seen other troopers hanging in trees with throats cut - Also heard that flame throwers were used. The Germans watched the Medics to find Aid stations & then hit them with mortars.[3]

One of the better-known battles the glider pilots were engaged in was the "Battle of Burp Gun Corner." During Operation Varsity in March of 1945, a crossroads was being held by some forty American glider pilots when several hundred German infantrymen, preceded by two tanks, attacked in the middle of the night. The glider pilots let the tanks approach before knocking out the first one with a bazooka;

---

2 F/O W.V. Stahlman, Handwritten Report, 437th TCG 84th TCS, RG 18, Entry #7, Federal Records Center, Suitland, Md. F/O Stahlman was the glider copilot who filed the report. He stated at the top that the pilot F/O Zumwalt was reported as okay but had not returned.
3 F/O J.A. Mahe & D.F. O' Hora, 85th TCS, Project 745005, RG18 Entry #7, Federal Records Center, Suitland, Md.

the second one turned and ran. This left the German infantry wide open. In the ensuing fight, the glider pilots killed over thirty men and took seventy prisoners.[4]

That they had proved themselves, although with the loss of many lives, was reflected in the treatment they began to receive. The difference was enough to warrant inclusion in a report by Flight Officer Harold T. Kennedy after VARSITY.

> The airborne took us out for evacuation on Sunday (25 March 1945) at 1330 hours. We were treated with respect as Officer[s] and Glider Pilot by the airborne during the whole operation.[5]

Flight Office Hoehne reported how General Ridgeway also recognized the successes of the glider pilots.

> That night we returned to guard the CP and we slept in turns. The next morning (Thursday) four of us (F/O Edinger, F/O Word and another man and myself) went out to search gliders for jeeps, ammunition, etc., and also for water as were out of it. We got lots of ammunition and a machine gun but no water. When we got back General Ridgeway had a formation for the glider pilots and commended us on the excellent job we had done.[6]

Regardless of these and many other successful exploits reported back to AAF headquarters, there was little else in the way of acknowledgment of the glider pilots' actions. More than once, they left a first aid station to make way for a more seriously wounded airborne soldiers. They administered first aid under fire to airborne

---

4 Milton Dank, *The Glider Gang*, 253.
5 F/O Harold T. Kennedy, 437th TCG 85th TCS,"TCMICS-GP," RG 18, Entry #7, Federal Records Center, Suitland, Md.
6 F/O A.W. Hoehne and F/O A.B. May, 437th TCG 85th TCS, "Glider Pilot Interrogation," RG 18 Entry #7, Federal Records Center, Suitland, Md.

and glider pilot alike, either alone or with other Allied soldiers on the ground. Many times, they pulled a victim to safety at risk of their own lives:

> We carried a trailer, ammo and 6 A/B. Our approach was hindered by poor visibility (300 yds.). SA fire was heavy and we hit the dirt. One A/B was wounded in the leg, and another hit on the head. A third was hit in the back of the neck and on the hand. I was wounded slightly in the left side but it was not necessary for me to report to the aid station. . . . I went to the 194th CP and took first aid men back to the wounded near the glider. I returned to the CP then proceeded to the 680th FA CP and reported to Captain Hobbs. Remained there 36 hours and acted as part of 2nd line of defense. [7]

After a rough landing, Flight Officer Whipple and the men he was with joined up with glider pilots to free another glider pilot trapped under the wing of his glider.

> Came in short, dumped it over trees, came down and started pulling out, came in on nose wheel. Put brakes on before landing. On impact elevator came off and undercarriage. Went in on skids. Skids collapsed up through fuselage between jeep and gun and helped hold them in. Ground looped the glider, gun and jeep held. . . . After landing got the tail off parts of the glider strung out 200 feet behind. Got jeep out. Nose mashed up. . . . Glider was total wash out. Didn't get out of the field that night. Hid the gun under the hedgerow along field. Didn't know where anything was. Scouted along road, went over into field across the road, helped F/O's Buchanan and Mack who landed in next field. There were airborne along the road. We were told

---

7 2nd Lt. Matthew P. Reilly and 2nd Lt. Melvin H. Spachman, 439th TCG 93rd TCS, "TCMICS-GP," RG 18 Entry #7, Federal Records Center, Suitland, Md.

> to stick with them. Ran into 2nd Lt. Burrus, F/O's Lafferty, Harts, Kane, McPherren, Lancaster, Hogan and G.L. King. Fowler went about half a mile southwest and helped get a wing off of a glider pilot down there whose name was Harry Lee, seriously injured. Went to report to first aid and when we went back later he was gone. Stayed under cover near field where landed all night. Next morning King was talking to Lt. Hart, platoon commander, and he thought we were surrounded, 300 to 400 yards from enemy lines. Wanted someone to go back and get help for Mack and Buchanan who were injured and to report position. Left about 0630 with McPherron, King, and Whipple and got to Les Forges, regimental command post and gave information to a Colonel there. Met medical captain and he got outfit up to Buchanan and Mack. Think Buchanan had a broken leg and Mack had face lacerations, injuries to hands and arms. . . Saw Nelson, glider pilot 441st Group (?) dead beside barn at Les Forges. About 2,000 all glider pilots went to beach, fired on by snipers. . . . [8]

The crew from a tow plane shot down during the Invasion of Holland was joined by Flight Officer Wilson, whose glider had landed in another field. Together, they attempted to get to a glider and provide a first aid kit to treat a badly burned glider pilot.

> The crew-chief and pilot landed in one field and were joined by the radio operator who had landed in an adjoining field. A glider, other than the one they were towing, was seen in a nearby field. The three joined a group of Airborne personnel and F/O Wilson, 36th T.C. Sq., who was the glider pilot. The three crew members and the glider pilot went over to the glider to get first-aid equipment to treat the glider pilot's face

---

8 F/O Whipple and F/O Jas. Fowler, 437th TCG 83rd TCS, "Glider Pilot Interrogation," RG 18 Entry #7, Federal Records Center, Suitland, Md.

and hands, which were severely burned. Before reaching the glider, however, they were pinned down by sniper fire from a nearby farmhouse.[9]

It took about thirty minutes to finally reach the first aid pack and administer first aid. However, it took a joint effort of the tow plane crew, F/O Wilson, and airborne personnel that came upon them and provided cover fire. The glider pilots were often engaged in combat prior to and during the time they were helping injured soldiers or setting up aid stations, equipment, and supplies for which they often flew in.

> We were subject to heavy sniper fire as soon as we landed. My load consisting of a hospital jeep, a Capt. and three enlisted men was out almost before we had stopped. Copilot and myself took cover in a ditch until from snipers had subsided. We helped clear a house of about 20 German prisoners and we then set up a temporary first aid station. We helped guard the prisoners. We helped bring out 4,000 prisoners under Col. Dukenson.[10]

Some mission reports list few glider pilot injuries, while others list numerous injuries. Much of this can be accounted for by the weather they were flying and landing in, the amount of enemy resistance they encountered, and the landing zone conditions. Too often, however, glider pilots sustained substantial injuries upon landing before moving into combat or administering first aid to others. Flight Officer Kenneth MC Grath's report reflects a head injury, fractures, and multiple torn muscles sustained from the landing alone.

---

9   Office of the Intelligence Officer, "Report on Lost Aircraft," 36th TCS, 316th TCG AAF, September 25, 1944. RG 18 Entry #7, Federal Records Center, Suitland, Md.

10   F/O D. Parrot 437th TCG 84th TCS, "TCMICS-GP," RG 18 Entry #7, Federal Records Center, Suitland, Md.

> After release had to make a turn over the flak installations and felt hits in the wings. In landing I had to fly under the power lines and make a low turn into the field and in doing so was unable to get my left wing up. The left wing hit and that is the last I remember until I regained consciousness. After regaining consciousness, I found myself upside down in the glider. I got out and then got the copilot out and treated the cut on his forehead. I then got an aid man and had him taken to the aid station along with the Airborne Lieutenant who had several cuts about the face and possible a fractured ankle. I then went to the rear behind the aid station and stayed until the next afternoon when I discovered that I was unable to get around so I reported to the aid station and was sent to the hospital. I had mussles torn loose in my left arm and both legs.[11]

The injuries sustained by the glider pilots and glider infantry alike resulted in injured personnel needing the immediate assistance of others and protection from the enemy. Flight Officer John Martins made sure the injured in his glider were as safe as could be and received food and medical aid. He then went on to knock out machine gun nests.

> There was considerable machine gun fire at this time, and we finally landed in a field right in the DZ O, and got to the ground okay. One skid came off, and we finally stopped in a ditch, by the edge of the field. The jeep broke loose (5 hoists gave way) and went into ditch, the nose of glider flew up & the jeep stopped directly below us. The ammunition, radio Eq. & small Eq. slid forward & pinned the two passengers to the dash. Both received possible leg fractures. We unloaded the Eq. that was against the two passengers & then carried them over to

---

11   F/O Kenneth T. MC Grath, D.S. 437th TCG 83rd TCS, "TCMICS-GP," RG 18 Entry #7, Federal Records Center, Suitland, Md.

the next field, and hid them in the hedge row & gave each a shot of morphine. We looked to see if any enemy was around, then took food & water to the two injured persons, then we took off for the main road 9:00 A.M. At 9:30 we contacted para troopers & AB we asked for help, & they said they would send help back. F/O May went with them. F/O Martins went back to watch the injured & at 1200 two jeeps came to take the gun from the glider in adjoining field. At that time one of the jeeps took the gun and the other jeep took the two injured AB back to (hospital) farmhouse, which was giving first aid. We asked the jeep to come back and pickup F/O Keough, Joseph copilot, F/O Dan Lombard F/O pilot, sprained foot. Keough broken left leg & right arm & was suffering a great deal who had one of morphine. The jeeps came back & took Keough to get first aid. F/O Lombard had walked to the farmhouse. . . . Then I (Martins) dug in & about 5:00PM I was asked to be a runner, by the airborne from one C.P. (defending bridge) to main C.P. located near orchard, near the South side of the drop zone. . . . Then I went back to my own C.P. We went to the swamp to pick up food rations & were fired (a barrage) upon, couldn't dig in, so we took off with a half case of rations. Being fired upon continuously. Heavy barrage was laid down upon C.P. all evening until 2nd lift came in. Then they lifted barrage & tried to fire on the gliders & towplane. .88 fire & machine gun fire. About 12:00 P.M. they brought fire back on C.P. Next morning the C.P. & 4 fields to the East was evacuated & again heavy fire was encountered, but no damage, No one hit or injured. Then we started back to the beach . . . we turned the prisoners over to the MP's & we also turned over all Eq. we had left to the ground forces (who had lost all their Eq. in landing). When I left with the paratroopers, we stopped from time to time to knock out machine gun nests (2 or 3). Then I came to a Italian C.P. and inquired for the div. C.P. I & four F/O took off for div. C.P. & were shot on several times. I helped guard an outpost, prisoners and helped out all I could. . . . Injured - F.O Keough - leg & arm fracture or broken, F/O Lombard -injured foot - sprained, F/O Roger Markley - broken leg & swollen bad, 1st Lt. Laird/ F/O Kuller - were ahead of us but we did not see anything of them. F/O May Wm. K. and F/O Lauri - were behind never saw them.[12]

Many glider pilots received aid from other glider pilots and were able to walk out and continue to fight, while others left the aid stations so the more seriously wounded could be cared for.

All were hit by small arms fire after landing, Lt. Gabriel in the arm, Lt. Hillas in the shoulder, and Lt. Morian in the temple, a superficial wound. Lt. Hagee was hit in the face by the glider control post in landing. His lip was badly cut, but both he and Lt. Morian left the aid station against orders to make room for the more seriously injured airborne personnel. Lt. Hagee made the trek back to the evacuation station on foot with other members of his squadron. When Lt. Hillas was hit, 2nd Lt. Aurel F. Grgasevich, his copilot, left cover and administered first aid under enemy fire.[13]

However, it was, at times, difficult for the glider pilots to get medical attention they needed. Arguments ensued over whose responsibility it was to medically tend to the glider pilots, a position that had not been assigned by the Air Corps. Again, this appears to have varied according to the group the glider pilots were assigned to; however, there were consequences for those injured, as reported by Lt. Brewer manning the front lines in Market.

---

12   F/O John S. Martins & F/O Joseph E. May, 437th TCG, Handwritten Report, Normandy, RG 18 Entry #7, Federal Records Center, Suitland Md.
13   "Casualties," 314th TCG Serial A-22, Varsity Mission, RG 18 Entry # 7, Federal Records Center, Suitland Md.

I believe that the glider pilots of our Group were not led as well as they could have been. In future missions better leadership should be provided... No medical personnel were assigned to the glider pilots and it was five hours before one of our wounded men was assisted. There seemed to be some argument as to who should take care of him.[14]

THE 3 B'S

Hitler's original tactical vision for the airborne to deliver men and troops behind the enemy worked well for the Allied forces who adopted it. The glider pilots were ultimately responsible for the sustenance of the airborne troops and their weapons through the direct delivery of the troops and the 3 B's of War—beans, bullets, and Band-Aids—without which a mission would not have been possible, never mind successful. The amounts the gliders flew in speaks volumes about their contributions to the war and the important part gliders played. In the Invasion of Southern France alone, gliders flew in 400 gallons of gasoline, 191,046 lbs. of ammunition, 11,483 lbs. of rations. In the Invasion of Normandy, they carried in 280 gallons of gasoline, 202,062 lbs. of ammunition, and 5,672 lbs. of rations. During the Invasion of Holland, they carried 1,535 gallons of gasoline, 520,331 lbs. of ammunition; 70,634 lbs. of rations.

In Bastogne, where the American and German bodies were stacked in separate piles, twelve to a pile, a young girl named Monique Guiot recorded that the Americans were running out of supplies fast. "They believe it is all over for them and us," she recorded in her diary.[15] A doctor recorded, "Patients with head wounds or injuries to the chest or abdomen are awaiting a slow death because they

---

14   2nd Lt. Clinton Brewer, 439th TCG 93rd TCS, "Glider Pilot Report," Reports, RG 18 Entry #7, Federal Records Center, Suitland, Md.
15   "The Siege of Bastogne Up Close and Personal," Yale University Press, December 3, 2014, www.yearbooks.yale.edu/2014/12/03/the-siege-of-bastogne- up- close-and-personal/, December 3, 2014/.

cannot be operated on."[16] Into this maelstrom of death, glider pilots flew to provide relief to their fellow soldiers while General Patton brought in the line forces. They dispatched, from December 22 to December 27, 61 gliders carrying 184,740 lbs. of equipment, and nine critically needed medical personnel to aid the 101st Airborne, which were the first to arrive, all flown by glider pilots that volunteered for the mission despite the odds against their coming back.[17] The breakdown by cargo between December 23 to December 27 was the following: 86 lbs. of rations, 2,975 gallons of gasoline, 106,291 lbs. of ammunition. and 32,823 lbs. of combat equipment and supplies.[18] Another 45,540 lbs. of ammunition were lost in gliders that were shot down, crashed, or destroyed on the landing zone.[19] Further analysis would need to be done to see if these were the gliders that received the wrong intelligence concerning the corridor to fly in and if they were also the gliders the missing in action glider pilots were flying.

In the China Burma India Theater, the first night of Broadway, gliders brought in approximately 530 personnel, 3 mules, and 29,972 pounds of stores.[20] On March 5, an additional 153 personnel and 2,400 pounds of stores were delivered.[21] The numbers attest to the

---

16   The Siege of Bastogne Up Close and Personal.
17   Statistical Control, "Resupply to 101st Airborne Division - DZ- Bastogne, Belgium (22nd to 27the December 1944) Gliders," Statistical Analysis, Microfilm Collection 546.287-1, Air Force Historical Research Agency, Maxwell AFB.
18   Statistical Control, "Resupply to 101st Airborne Division - DZ- Bastogne, Belgium (22nd to 27the December 1944): Analysis of Supplies and Equipment Dropped and Landed on DZ or LZ - Gliders," Statistical Analysis, Microfilm Collection 546.287-1, Air Force Historical Research Agency, Maxwell AFB.
19   Statistical Control, "Resupply to 101st Airborne Division, Bastogne, Belgium and Units at Marcoury, Belgium (22nd to 27the December 1944): Percent of Casualty by Crew Positions," Statistical Analysis, Microfilm Collection 546.287-1, Air Force Historical Research Agency, Maxwell AFB.
20   Historical Data: Army Air Force, India, Burma Sector, China Burma India Theater, "1st Air Commando Invasion of Burma," 1st Air Commandos, BO681. 4, Air Force Historical Research Agency, Maxwell AFB. The number of personnel looks to read 530, however the typeface is not clear so that figure may not be correct.
21   Historical Data: Army Air Force, India, Burma Sector, China Burma India Theater, "1st Air Commando Invasion of Burma," 1st Air Commandos, BO681. 4, Air Force Historical Research Agency, Maxwell AFB.

massive amounts of supplies the glider pilots, with the aid of their tow pilots, delivered to further the Allied war effort.

The true impact of the supplies, weapons, and personnel ferried in by the glider pilots cannot be overstated. Without the gasoline brought in by the glider pilots, the ground forces would have been unable to operate their equipment or move themselves out of harm's way. All movement would have ceased, and all evacuations would have been on foot or by whatever means could be commandeered. Ground personnel would have been exceedingly vulnerable, and any forward momentum would have undoubtedly ground to a halt. Countless times, the airborne were low or out of ammunition; not only did the glider pilots bring in ammunition, but they also returned to hot landing zones to grab ammunition and deliver it to ground troops so they could continue to fight. One cannot wage an effective war against armed enemy troops without weapons and ammunition, and the amounts brought in certainly could not have been brought in on the ground troops or paratrooper's persons. Many wounded could not have been treated without the medical supplies and equipment for first aid setups, and inevitably, many would have had their wounds terribly infected or died. Often, glider pilots were without rations and water despite bringing in huge quantities of food to feed the fighting and hungry, exhausted troops. The cargo the gliders carried were lifesaving supplies that gave the Allies the upper hand in the war and extended the most critical of needs in any war—the supply line.

COMMENDATIONS

The glider pilots have been painted as a wild group of carousing men who were cavalier and independent. Yet the remainder of their portrait has not been so fully broadcast. These men fully realized the nature of the missions they were embarking on, and the stress took a physical and mental toll on them. Martin Wolfe recounts one small example:

Just prior to our mission across the Rhine River at Wesel several of us were sitting and jawing in the tent. I noticed Herb Christie [glider pilot] was in terrible distress. When he tried to talk, only one side of his mouth and one side of his face would move. We rushed him to Doc Coleman. He explained that because of the accumulated stress from all out missions and the preparation for the Rhine crossing, Herb's central nervous system had simply rebelled. The doctors said it was like an electrical system had shorted out. But Herb recovered and he went on the Rhine mission. [22]

Before a mission, some gambled, some wrote letters home, some drank, and some sat in solitude. Those who were fresh from training and untried in an actual mission have recounted how they were anxious to prove themselves yet were sobered by the quiet and still demeanor of those glider pilots who had flown and survived multiple missions and who understood the reality that death was coming for some of them in just a matter of hours, wondering if this was their last mission. Yet time and again, they climbed in their gliders, reassured the troops they were ferrying, and flew into battle just as the tow pilots, bombers, and fighter pilots did. Despite the equally, if not more dangerous, nature of their job, the glider pilots received very few official commendations during the course of the war. Those few that were written speak for themselves. A commendation passed down from headquarters of the IX TCC on July 5, 1944, to the glider pilots of various TCG, commented on their splendid performance:

> As Troop Carrier glider pilots, these officers meritoriously climaxed a most successful program of intensive, specialized training and joint maneuvers with airborne units in aerial flights by their superb performance in the initial Troop Carrier phases

---

22   Wolfe, Martin, *Green Light! Men of the 81st Troop Carrier Squadron Tell Their Story*, (Philadelphia: University of Pennsylvania Press,1989), 147.

of the invasion of the European continent. The magnificent spirit and enthusiasm displayed by these officers, combined with skill, courage and devotion to duty is reflected in their brilliant operation of unarmed gliders of light construction, at minimum altitudes and air speeds, in unfavorable weather conditions, over water, and into the face of vigorous enemy opposition, with no possibility of employing evasive action, and in their successful negotiation of hazardous landings in hostile territory, to spearhead the Allied invasion of the continent. Their respective duty assignments were performed in such an admirable manner as to produce exceptional results in the greatest and most successful airborne operation in the history of world aviation.[23]

Although less official, the following excerpt was not shown to the men involved but included in the composite narrative of 62nd TCS:

> The 314th Tr Carr Gp Glider Officer particularly asked that it be noted in this report that the courage, discipline, and general conduct of all glider personnel of this unit and Group were superb, and that all personnel acted in an extremely laudable way. No difficulties of delay, "gold-bricking", failure to carry out orders with promptness and dispatch or other military or personal faults were encountered.[24]

Included in the same report was a tribute to Captain Emil M. Crozier who was "shot in [the] back and killed after landing, having been wounded in the air first, and further injured when glider crashed

---

23 HQ IX TCC, General Orders Number 33, Microfilm Collection 546.287-1, Air Force Historical Research Agency, Maxwell AFB.
24 Captain Morrison Loesch, "Composite Narrative of the Operation, Compiled from Reports of 62nd Tr Carr Sqn Glider Personnel," RG 18 Entry #7, Commendations, 3, Federal Records Center, Suitland, Md.

into [the] ground."²⁵ This was followed by, "It is to be noted in this connection that before his death Capt Crozier exhibited great gallantry and courage in assisting to release wounded personnel in his glider, while he himself was under sniper and other ground fire at the same time."²⁶

In spite of his earlier letter citing problems with the glider pilots, General James M. Gavin also commented on the successful glider landings following Operation MARKET-GARDEN in a personal letter to Brigadier General Harold Clark:

> Our parachute drops and glider landings were the best in the history of the Division. The courageous performance of your pilots has been the admiration of all of us. Thank you very much for all that you have done for us . . . ²⁷

Brigadier General Paul L. Williams, commanding general of the IX TCC, further commented on General Ridgeway's previous praise of the glider pilots and TCC operations after the Invasion of Normandy.

> Receipt of the foregoing communication is highly gratifying and is ample testimony of the appreciation of the 82nd Division for the magnificent efforts of the units transporting the Division. The fact that General RIDGEWAY, under stress of battle, felt it necessary to forward basic letter is particularly pleasing, and will serve as additional evidence of his appreciation of a task well performed. To all, combat crews and ground personally, you have made an individual contribution to the outstanding success of this Command. The basic letter needs no expanding,

---

25 Loesch, "Composite Narrative of the Operation, Compiled from Reports of 62nd Tr Carr Sqn Glider Personnel," 1.
26 Loesch, 1.
27 Brig. Gen. James M. Gavin, Personal Letter to Brig. Gen. Harold Clark, commanding general 52nd TCW, 313th TCG, Market, Sept. 1944, Commendations, RG 18 Entry #7, Federal Records Center, Suitland, Md.

and, accordingly, I may only add my sincere appreciation for your loyalty, zeal and devotion to duty.[28]

Despite their lack of official commendations, the glider pilots earned the respect and gratitude of those they delivered safely into battle. A letter written to the glider pilots of the 95th TCS by an airborne soldier, Captain Andrew J. Hawkins, Jr., can tell us more about the type of men the glider pilots were and the job they did than any number of books, reports, suppositions, or commendations:

> For some time I have intended writing to tell you how much every man of my Battery appreciate the swell job you did in bringing us in on the "Invasion of Holland". In case you don't know we had all six guns in position and ready to fire two hours after the landing. The only equipment lost was in the one glider shot down before it reached the "L-Z". Our losses in men were so small it is almost unbelievable. All of this we attribute to your skill and determination in flying us in and on the landing. The Battery is still doing well and we have shot twice as much ammunition as we did in Normandy. We, like you, hope that there won't be another mission in this theater, however if there is one we hope we will be fortunate enough to have you take us in.[29]

The feeling from the glider pilots toward the airborne was mutual:

> I have nothing but praise for the 17th A/B.[30]

---

28 Brigadier General Paul L. Williams, Headquarters IX Troop Carrier Command to Distribution "B", Loss Stations and Staff Sections, June 15, 1944.
29 Capt. Andrew J. Hawkins, FA, Comdg., Battery B 319th Glider Field Artillery Battalion, Letter to Glider Pilots 95th TCS, Nov. 21, 1944, 95th TCS, "Market" Mission 9/44, Commendations RG18 Entry #7, Federal Records Center, Md.
30 Lt. Louis L. Hiti, 437th TCG, 84th TCS, "TCMIS-GP," RG 18 Entry #7, Federal Records Center, Suitland, Md.

> Landing was very successful under the circumstances. One of the airborne wounded before landing and the other killed in climbing out of the glider. Wounded man was administered first aid and in my opinion the airborne troops did a marvelous job in breaking down enemy resistance as quickly as possible.[31]

The war is long past, and few glider pilots are still surviving, and yet unlike the airborne and the power pilots, their place in history has never been fully secured. It is not too late to correct history and keep the legacy alive for the suicide jockeys of WWII. The glider pilots were and are a testament to their ability to not only survive but succeed when tested despite political gamesmanship. Perhaps General Westmoreland said it best:

> The intrepid pilots who flew the gliders were as unique as their motorless flying machines. Never before in history had any nation produced aviators whose duty it was to deliberately crash land and then go on to fight as combat infantrymen. They were no ordinary fighters. Their battlefields were behind enemy lines. Every landing was a genuine do-or-die situation for the glider pilots. It was their awesome responsibility to repeatedly risk their lives by landing heavily laden aircraft containing combat soldiers and equipment in unfamiliar fields deep within enemy-held territory, often in total darkness. They were the only aviators during World War II who had no motors, no parachutes and no second chances.[32]

Despite the honor it was to receive the appreciation of those in

---

31 F/O Max I. Morrison and F/O Karle A. Gearhart, 437th TCG 85th TCS ,"TCMIS-GP," RG18 Entry #7, Federal Records Center, Suitland, Md.
32 RN3DB: Robert Novells's Third Dimension Blog, "Who Are The Aviators Who Wear The Silver Wings With The Letter 'G'," March 3, 2017, https://www.robertnovell.com/who-are-the-aviators-who-wear-the-silver-wings-with-the-letter-g-march-3-2017/.

higher commands, at the end of the day, they fought and survived alone, and so it is only fitting that this book, which begins with words from one of their own, also end that way. As to their success and survival, Lt. William T. Owens summed it up in one small sentence:

> It depended to a great extent on the ingenuity and experience of the pilots.[33]

---

33   Lt. William T. Owens, 427th TCG, 86th TCS, "TCMIGS-EEPCM," RG18 Entry #7, Federal Records Center Suitland, Md.

ACKNOWLEDGMENTS

There are so many people who deserve my deepest gratitude, who helped with research of this book, and who made it possible. First, I would like to thank Mark Vlahos, who, through his kindness and encouragement, led me to the option of publishing *Suicide Jockeys*. An author in his own right, he was very giving with his time, expertise, and encouragement. I would also like to thank Jim Pollard, Lt. Col. US Army ret., and his wife, Nita Pollard, who not only read my manuscript but shared it with other experts in the field. Their kindness in sharing it with other experts in military studies opened several doors to additional perspectives of the airborne in WWII.

The expertise of Lawson MacGruder III, Lt. Gen. US Army ret., Leonard J. Fullenkamp, Col. US Army ret., Timothy Jones, Lt. Col US Army ret., Christopher Hossfeld, Col. US Army ret., and Dr. Thomas Hatfield was invaluable to my work. My deepest thanks to them. I would like to thank Charles Day, an expert on the CG-4A, for the technical information he provided, Sharon McCullar, curator of the Silent Wings Museum and former curator Don Abbe, also of the Silent Wings Museum, for answering questions about the glider construction. Also, Gary Stripling, the National World War II Glider Pilot Association research team manager, for taking the time to search through databases to locate information. It is the small, detailed information they shared that is so important for accuracy.

Above all, I would like to thank my husband, Robert Taylor, who has supported me and enabled my research into the World War II glider pilots for many years. My sisters, Michele Mousseau and Suzanne Brown, who have helped get *Suicide Jockeys* out to the public. To all my friends who have supported me regardless of what new destination I had in mind, who read my manuscript, and whose suggestions were excellent, thank you. But most of all, to my father, Paul W. Mousseau Sr., and all the glider and tow pilots who provided so much information and approved of the manuscript when it was initially done as my thesis. To those great men, who showed me unfailing kindness and supplied endless information, I am eternally grateful. I hope I did them justice.

This book would not be in print without Greg Fields, author and acquisitions editor at Koehler Books, Miranda Dillon, who patiently did numerous edits, Lauren Sheldon with her knowledge of gliders that did the graphic design, and John Koehler, owner of Koehler Books. The glider pilots and I extend them a special thanks for fulfilling Flight Officer Rhodes's request and for stepping forward to reserve a place in history for the "Boys in the CG-4As." We thank you from the bottom of our hearts.

SELECTED BIBLIOGRAPHY

Listed here is a selection of the many books I have read and sources I have consulted over the years of my research of the glider pilot program. In many cases, they are about the war itself, but a clear understanding of the larger picture is necessary to understand how the glider pilots operated within the Army Air Forces. It is impossible to understand the glider pilot, their importance, and their successes through the study of them through a microscope. I have included excellent sources that I strongly recommend to anyone wishing to delve deeper into the subject.

The record collections that I originally located at Bolling AFB have now been transferred to the Air Force Historical Research Agency at Maxwell AFB. I have updated the location accordingly after speaking to staff at the Agency. I have kept the original citations but do not know if they have been reorganized since the transfer.

BOOKS

Ambrose, Stephen E. *Pegasus Bridge, June 6, 1944*. New York: Simon and Schuster, 1985.

Angelucci, Enzo. *Rand McNally encyclopedia of Military Aircraft 1914 to the Present*, New York: Gallery Books, 1990.

Armed Forces Office of Air Force History, *The Army Air Forces in World War II*. Washington D.C.: U.S. Government Printing Office, 1983.

Beeson, Colin R. *The Glider Pilot War at Home and Overseas*. Manhattan: Kansas State University, 1978.

Best, Gary A., *Silent Invaders: Combat Gliders of the Second World War,* England: Fonthill Media Limited, 2014.

Blair, Clay. *Ridgway's Paratroopers: The American Airborne in World War II.* New York: William Morrow & Co., 1985.

Breuer, William B. *Drop Zone Sicily: The First Airborne Strike on Fortress Europe.* Novato Calif.: Presidio Press, 1983; reprint, New York: Jove Books, 1985.

Burgett, Donald R. *Curahee!* Boston: Houghton Mifflin Cambridge, Mass.: Riverside Press, 1967.

Carter, Ross S. *Those Devils in Baggy Pants.* New York: New American Library, 1951.

Colby, C. B. *Fighting Gear of World War II: Equipment and Weapons of the American G.I.* New York: Coward-Mccann, 1961.

Congdon, Don, ed. *Combat WWII: European Theater of Operations.* With a Foreword by Herbert Mitgang. New York: Arbor House, 1983.

Crouch, Howard R. *U.S. Small Arms of World War 2: A Guide for the Collector, Shooter, & Historian.* Falls Church, Va.: SCS Publications, 1984.

Dank, Milton. *The Glider Gang: An Eyewitness History of World War II Glider Combat.* New York: J.B. Lippincott, 1977.

Devlin, Gerard M. *Silent Wings: The Saga of the u. S. Army and Marine Combat Glider Pilots During World War II.* With a Foreword by Lieutenant General Sir Napier Crookenden. Introduction by General William C. Westmoreland. New York: St. Martin's Press, 1985.

Diagram Group. *Weapons: An International Encyclopedia from 500 B.C. to 2000 A.D.* New York: St. Martin's Press, 1980.

Edward, Roger. *German Airborne Troops 1936-1945.* With a Foreword by Generaloberst Kurt Student. Garden City, N.Y.: Doubleday, 1974.

Ellis John. *The Sharp End: The Fighting Man in World War II.* New York: Charles Scribner's Sons, 1980.

Farrar-Hockley, Brigadier Antony H. *Airborne Carpet: Operation Market Garden.* Edited by David Mason. New York: Ballantine, 1969. Nashville Tenn.: Salton Battery Press, 1980.

Fenelon, James M. *Four Hours of Fury,* New York, N.Y.: Scribner, 2019.

Glantz, Lieutenant Colonel David M. *The Soviet Airborne Experience.* Fort Leavenworth, Kan.: U.S. Army Command and General Staff College, 1984.

Guild, Frank Jr. *Action of the Tiger: The Saga of the 437th TCG.* Nashville, Tenn: Battery Press, 1980.

Hogg, Ian V. *The Complete Illustrated Encyclopedia of the World's Firearms.* New York: A & W Publishers, 1978.

Military Pistols and Revolvers: *The Handguns of the Two World Wars.* New York: Arco Publishing, 1970.

Huston, James A. *Out of the Blue: U.S. Army Airborne Operations in World War II.* West Lafayette, Ind.: Purdue University Studies, 1972.

Katcher Philip. *The U.S. Army 1941-45.* Men-At-Arms Series, ed. Martin Windrow. London: Osprey Publishing, 1984.

MacDonald, Charles. *Airborne.* New York: Ballantine, 1970.

Mrazek, James E. *Fighting Gliders of World War II.* New York: St. Martin's Press, 1977.

Office of Air Force History. *Air Force Combat Units of World War II.* Edited by Maurer Maurer. With a Foreword by Richard H. Kohn. Washington D.C.: Government Printing Office, 1961; reprint, Washington, D.C.: Office of Air Force History, 1983.

Perna, Dr. Albert F., Lt. Col. USAF (Ret.). *The Glider Gladiators (of World War II).* Freeman, S.D.: Pine Hill Press, 1970.

Ryan, Cornelius. *A Bridge Too Far.* New York: Simon and Schuster, 1974.

Sweeting, C. G. *Combat Flying Clothing Vol. 2, Army Air Forces Clothing During World War II.* Washington, D.C.: Smithsonian Institution Press, 1984.

Combat Flying Equipment: U.S. Army Aviators' Personal Equipment, 1917-1945. With a Foreword by Donald S. Lopez. Washington, D.C.: Smithsonian Institution Press, 1989.

van Reken, Donald L. *The 32nd Troop Carrier Squadron: An Airborne C-47 Squadron 1942-1945: Pilots, Paratroops, and Gliders in North Africa, Sicily, England, France and Germany.* Holland, Mich.: By the author, 44 East 15th Street, 1989.

Van Wagner, R.D. *Any Place, Any Time, Any Where: First Commandos in World War II.* Atglen, Penn.: Shiffner Military/Aviation History, 1988.

Vlahos, Mark C. Col USAF (Ret.). *Leading the Way to Victory: A History of the 60th Troop Carrier Group 1940-1945.* New York: Knox Press, 2022.

Wolfe, Martin. *Green Light! Men of the 81st Troop Carrier Squadron Tell Their Story.* Philadelphia: University of Pennsylvania Press, 1989.

Wood, Alan. *History of the World's Glider Forces.* Northamptonshire, England: Patrick Stevens Limited, 1990.

PERIODICALS AND NEWSLETTERS

Clendenin, John, Sr. "'Crazy' Years as a Glider Pilot." Aerospace Historian, September 1976.

Conley, Manuel. "Silent Squadrons." American History, June 1983.

Du Bois, Arthur E. "Insignia of the United States Armed Forces." National Geographic, June 1942.

MacWilliam, J. H., and Bruce D. Callander. "The Third Lieutenants." Air Force Magazine, March 1990.

McCausey, B. J. "A Glider Named Hamilton's Reply." Aerospace History, December 1979.

Museum News. Terrell, Tx.: By the Military Glider Pilots Association, P.O. Box 775.

Newcomb, CMSgt. Harold, and Sgt. Russell W. Scmidt. "On Whispering Wings." Airman, May 1978.

On Tow. Conyers, Ga.: By the World War II Glider Pilots Association, 2559 Highway 138.

Silent Wings. Edited by William and Doris Horn. Dallas, Text: By the editors, 7038 Northaven Road.

INTERVIEWS AND CORRESPONDENCE

Bower, Lt. James E., USAF (Ret.), World War II glider pilot. Interview with author, October 1989, January 1990. Milledgeville, Ga.

Cook, Edward L., World War II glider pilot. Interview with author, August 1989, Tucson, Ariz.

Day, Charles, CG-4A Historian, email to author April 2023.

Garcia, Lt. Col. Herbert, USA (Ret.), curator, Tropical Lightning Museum. Interviews by the author, January 1990, February 1990, October 1990, Schofield Barracks, Ha.

Knickerbocker, William D., World War II glider pilot. Interview with author, September 1989, Midland, Tex.

McCullar, Sharon, Curator Silent Wings Museum, email with author February - April 2023.

Mortensen, Daniel R., Historian, Tactical Aviation, Office of Air Force History. Interview by the author, 19 April 1989, Bolling Air Force Base, Washington, D.C.

Mousseau, Lt. Col. Paul W., USAF (Ret.), World War II glider pilot. Interview by the author, 20 June 1989, Fresno, Calif.

Rosengrants, Col. David E., USAF (Ret.), World War II tow pilot. Interviews by the author, July 1989, September 1989, Abilene, Tex.

Sweeting, C. G., USAF (Ret.), retired curator of Flight Material at the National Air and Space Museum. Interviews by the author, September 1989, October 1989, Camp Springs, Md.

Taylor, Captain Jonathon Taylor, MV-22B Pilot, U.S. Marine Corps, interview by author, April 12, 2023, Washington D.C.

Wilmer, Douglas, World War II glider pilot. Interviews by the author, August 1989, Conyers, Ga.

COLLECTIONS

1st Commando A.F., "Medical History of the 1st Air Commandos" December 1944, Microfilm Collection, Air Force Historical Research Agency, Maxwell AFB.

Air Intelligence Contact Unit, Special Interviews, Microfilm Collection, Air Force Historical Research Agency, Maxwell AFB.

Assistant Chief of Air Staff, Intelligence, Historical Division. "Army Air Forces Historical Studies: No. 1, The Glider Pilot Training Program, 1941 to 1943." September 1943. Air Force Historical Research Agency, Maxwell AFB.

Carrier Aviation: Its Mission, Organization & Equipment." AAF School of Applied Tactics, AAF Tactical Center, Orlando, Fla., October 1944. Microfilm Collection. Air Force Historical Research Agency, Maxwell AFB.

Danielson, Lt. Col. Daniel W. Inf., "The Airborne Army: Organization and Employment." June 1945. Microfilm Collection. Air Force Historical Research Agency, Maxwell AFB.

Federal Records Center, Suitland, Md. Commendations. Federal Records Center, Suitland, Md. Record Group 18. Entry No. 7. Glider Pilot Interrogation Records.

Federal Records Center, Mission Reports. Record Group 18 Entry No. 7. Federal Records Center, Suitland, Md.

Headquarters IX Troop Carrier Command, "Consolidated Tactical Operations Summary Operations Neptune-Dragoon-Market," Statistical Control Office, Microfilm Collection, Air Force Historical Research Agency, Maxwell AFB.

Headquarters IX Troop Carrier Command, "General Orders Number 33," Microfilm Collection, Air Force Historical Research Agency, Maxwell AFB.

Kenneth Marts, Major, Troop Carrier Division Combat Operations Department, "Technical Considerations in the Employment of Military Gliders," March 1944. Microfilm Collection Air Force Historical Research Agency, Maxwell AFB.

George E. Peterson, Office of Flying Safety, Headquarters AAF, "Pilot Training Manual for the CG-4A Glider" 1945.

"Technical Considerations in the Employment of the Military Glider," March 1944. Microfilm Collection, Air Force Historical Research Agency, Maxwell AFB.

Wilson, Captain Wasson J. "Troop Carrier Aviation," December 3, 1943. Microfilm Collection. Air Force Historical Research Agency, Maxwell AFB.

DISSERTATION

McQuillen, John A., Jr. "American Military Gliders in World War II in Europe," Ph.D. diss., St. Louis University, 1975.

LEGISLATIVE

"Executive Order 9082 of March 3, 1942, Recognizing the Army of the United States and Transfers of Functions within the War Department"

National Security Act of 1947.50 U.S. Code §3001, July 26, 1947.

Pay Longevity Flight Officers, B-27373 , 22 Comp. Gen. 216 September 10,1942.

WEB PAGES

"Chindits Special Forces Burma: Operation Thursday the 2nd Chindit Expedition," 1944, https://www.chindits.info/Thursday/Operation Thursday.htm.

"Meet the U.S. Army's New Parachute," Aerospace America. March 1, 2020. https://aerospaceamerica.aiaa.org/departments/meet-the-u-s-armys-new-parachute/.

"Mission," Spencer, Leon Major USAF (Ret.), National World War II Glider Pilot Association. Accessed January 17, 2023, https://www.ww2gp.og/war/missions/.

Otensie, Ray, Air Force Material Command History Office, Air Force Material Command. Accessed September 16, 2019, https://www.wpafb.af.mil/News/Article-Display/Article/1961634/flashback-glidersfrom-wright-field-to-the-netherlands/

"Remagen," Hans den Brok, Author, Historian, National World War II Glider Pilot Association. Accessed December 15, 2023 https://www.ww2gp.org/remagen/.

"The Siege of Bastogne Up Close and Personal," Peter Schrijvers, December 3, 2014. 3https://yalebooks.yale.edu/2014/12/03/the-siege-of-bastogne-up-close-and-personal/.

"Was it the Air Corps of the Army Air Forces in WWII," Army Air Forces Historical Association. Accessed November 2022, http://www.aafha.org/air-corps-or-air-forces.html.

APPENDICES

APPENDIX A: USAAF RANKS DURING WORLD WAR II

The USAAF ranks during World War II descended as follows:[1]
- General
- Lieutenant General
- Major General
- Brigadier General
- Colonel
- Lieutenant Colonel
- Major
- Captain
- First Lieutenant
- Second Lieutenant
- Chief Warrant Officer
- Warrant Officer Junior Grade
- Flight Officer
- Master Sergeant 1st Grade
- First Sergeant 1st Grade
- Technical Sergeant 2nd Grade
- Staff Sergeant 3rd Grade
- Technician 3rd Grade
- Sergeant 4th Grade
- Technician 4th Grade
- Corporal 5th Grade
- Technician 5th Grade
- Private First-Class 6th Grade

---

1   Arthur E. Du Bois, "Insignia of the United States Armed Forces," National Geographic, June 1943.

APPENDIX B:
FLOW OF STUDENTS THROUGH GLIDER SCHOOLS

JUNE 15, 1942–SEPTEMBER 14, 1942

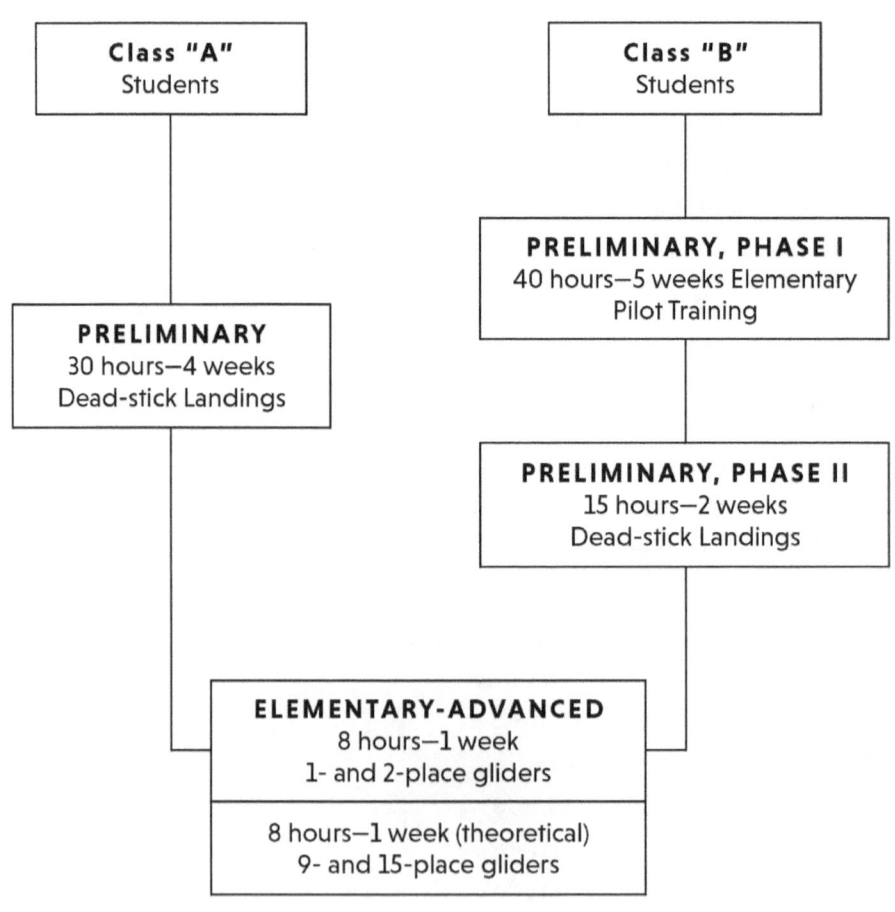

SEPTEMBER 14, 1942-FEBRUARY 26, 1943

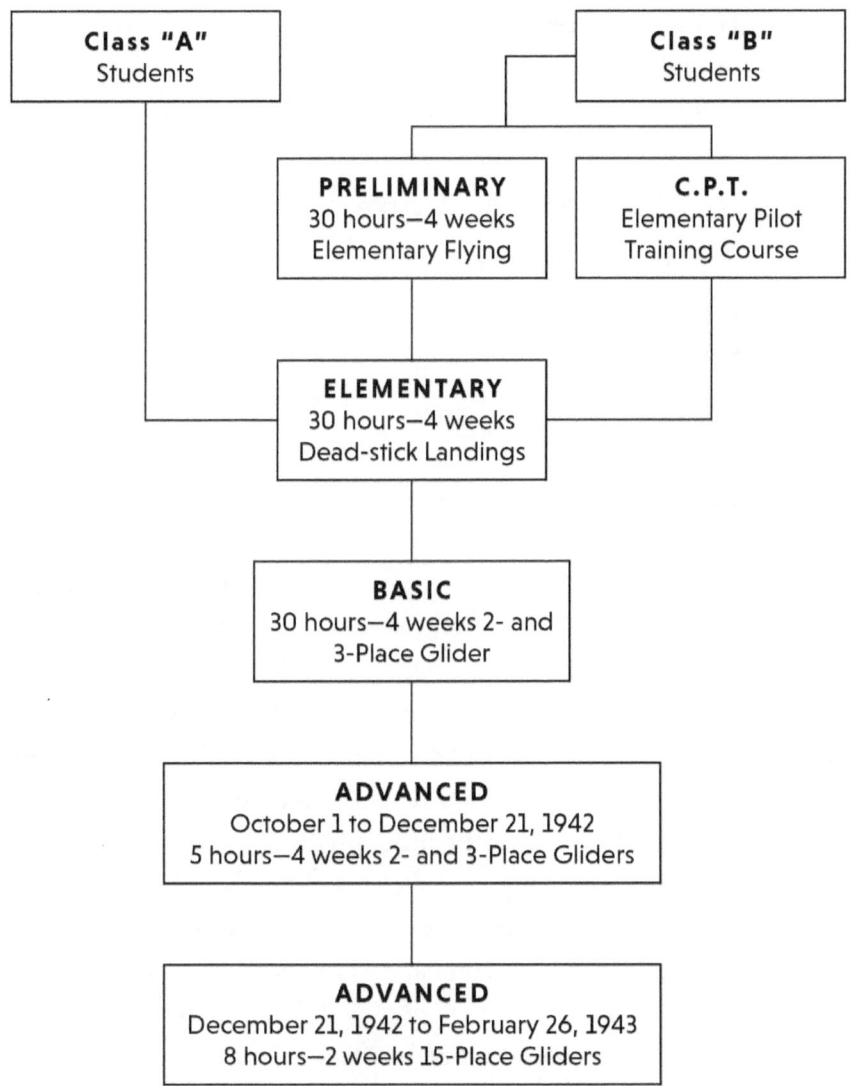

CLASS "A" STUDENTS

Aerial experience of one of the following types required:
1. Holder of currently effective airman certificate, private grade or higher.
2. Holder of a lapsed airman certificate, provided that such certificate did not lapse prior to January 1, 1941.
3. Having completed 200 or more glider flights.
4. Pilot training eliminees, provided they have fifty hours as principal pilot or student pilot in military or naval type aircraft.

CLASS "B" STUDENTS

No previous experience.

Because the aviation training of the glider pilots was part of The Glider Pilot Program, it reflected the same characteristic confusion and complexities. The constant alteration of pilot quotas had a direct effect on the aviation schools' abilities to handle the incoming students. Further delays were caused by glider manufacturing difficulties. Light power planes and soaring craft were used as glider substitutes, but it was discovered toward the end of the program that these did not give the pilots any real sense of flying a cargo glider, either loaded or unloaded, since the flight characteristics between the planes used for training and the cargo glider used in combat differed drastically. The absence of military experience in the field of gliders further handicapped the aviation instructors, who were unable to teach the tactical applications of the glider since they had not yet been developed. It was actually the first graduating students who flew the gliders into combat and refined the glider flying and landing techniques.

In May of 1942, the Glider Program was still lacking training gliders. To overcome this setback, a light plane training program was launched; its objective was for the graduates to be "qualified to operate light airplanes, and to make all landings with ignition off, both night and day, and to be qualified to service these airplanes in the field."[1] This Preliminary training lasted twenty days, with one and a half hours of flight instruction per day.[2] In its entirety, it involved the following:

Stalls and spins	2 hours
180° approaches with ignition turned off at 2,000 feet, practicing various approach patterns	4 hours
Various approaches with ignition turned off at 500, 1,000, 1,500, 2,000, and 3,000 feet	5 hours
Precision landings—no brakes	5 hours
Navigation of flight to point of strange field landing with ignition off at 5,000 feet	5 hours
Ignition off night landings from 2,000, 3,000, and 4,000 feet	5 hours

The remaining four hours were used for practicing rough areas.[3] The ground training segment consisted of an additional three hours per day and included the followed total times:

Meteorology	10 hours
Navigation	5 hours

---

1 Assistant Chief of Air Staff, Intelligence, Historical Division, "AAF Historical Studies: No. 1," September 1943, Bolling AFB Historical Research Library, Washington, D.C., 20. (Typewritten)
2 Assistant Chief of Air Staff, "AAF Historical Studies: No. 1," 21.
3 Assistant Chief of Air Staff, "AAF Historical Studies: No. 1," 21.

Maintenance	10 hours
Aircraft identification	2 hours
Chemical warfare defense	1 hour
Instruments	4 hours
Physical training	20 hours
Customs of the service, basic military training, and drill	8 hours[4]

There was, however, no method to check the quality of the instruction being received by the students, and it appears that any ground training given was very inadequate.[5]

The next phase was Elementary-Advanced training. From June 15, 1942, through September 14, 1942, ElementaryAdvanced followed Preliminary training. Beginning on September 14, 1942, and lasting until February 26, 1943, the Preliminary phase of training was renamed. It was then known as Elementary Training and the Elementary-Advanced Training was termed Basic Training. The Elementary-Advanced School consisted of two parts, each lasting one week. The total training days equaled ten days of 1 hour and fifty minutes per day.[6] The first portion, Elementary Training, was considered the "airplane gliding phase." It included the following:

Familiarization	1 hour
Precision landings	1 hour

---

4 Assistant Chief of Air Staff, "AAF Historical Studies: No. 1," 21.
5 Assistant Chief of Air Staff, "AAF Historical Studies: No. 1," 21.
6 Assistant Chief of Air Staff, "AAF Historical Studies: No. 1," 21.

Precision landings made from winch, pulley, or tow[7]	1 hour
Four airplane tows.	completed within 1 hour
Multiple airplane tows:	
By day	1:30
At night	2 hours[8]

The Advanced Training during the second week was never actually implemented, mainly because it was to familiarize the student with nine- and twelve-place gliders, which never reached the production stage. Its schedule was as follows:

Familiarization	1 hour
Precision landings/four in two hours on large gliders in single two position	
Multiple tows:	
By day	1 hour
At night	1 hour
Under the hood[9]	1 hour
During day with strange field precision landing after release at 5,000 feet	1 hour[10]

---

7 Towing the glider with an automobile was one of the initial methods used to get them airborne.
8 Assistant Chief of Air Staff, "AAF Historical Studies: No. 1," 21-22.
9 Blind flying.
10 Assistant Chief of Air Staff, "AAF Historical Studies: No. 1," 22.

The Elementary-Advanced ground school was scheduled as follows:

Simulated flying in Link Trainer[11]	5 hours
Radio equipment operation	2 hours
Maintenance	5 hours
Physical training	8 hours
Meteorology	5 hours
Soaring	5 hours
Glider characteristics and flying techniques	5 hours[12]

Class B students were required to take two phases of Preliminary Training before entering the Elementary-Advanced Training with the Class A students. Preliminary phase I involved forty hours of flight school over a period of twenty-five days, one hour and thirty-six minutes per day. The forty hours were split into nineteen hours of dual flight and twenty-one hours of solo flight. The ground school lasted seventy-five hours, and both segments were based on the Class A students' Preliminary Training.[13]

Preliminary training Phase II was a two-week course, totaling fifteen hours. In essence, it was a shortened version of the Class A Preliminary course on dead-stick landings. The phase I and phase II ground school training for Class B students equaled seventy-five hours, after which time the students were prepared to merge with the

---

11   The Link Trainer was basically a flight simulator used in World War II. It was never adjusted, however, to simulate the glider in flight. Lt. Col. Paul W. Mousseau (USAF Ret.), interview by author, 20 June 1989, Fresno, California.
12   Assistant Chief of Air Staff, "AAF Historical Studies: No. 1," 22.
13   Assistant Chief of Air Staff, "AAF Historical Studies: No. 1," 27.

Class A students.[14]

Because of fluctuations in the glider pilot recruitment program, adjustments became necessary in the aviation training schedules to graduate the maximum number of pilots. Weaknesses in the program were also becoming apparent. To rectify the situation, the Elementary-Advanced schools authorized the graduation of students without instrument training.

> As training progressed, certain weaknesses became evident in the curriculum. It would seem that there was not enough correlation between the preliminary glider and the glider schools. Student flying was suffering from inadequate instruction in signals and standard operating procedure. In flight training, insufficient time was being devoted to precision flying and strange field landings. In the ground school, the students were not taking an active enough part in the maintenance course. The Training Section of the Flying Training Command made an attempt to rectify these faults by directive, but some of the weaknesses in the training program must be attributed to inadequate material and training aids. For example, many of the schools were without instruments and therefore could not give the required hours in instrument training. The situation was recognized as unavoidable, and on August 26, the Elementary-Advanced schools were authorized to graduate students without instrument training.·[15]

On September 14, 1942, a new glider aviation program replaced the previous one. It was sixteen weeks long in its entirety and consisted of four stages: Preliminary, Elementary, Basic, and Advanced. Each course was taught at a different location and totaled four weeks. The only trainees required to take Preliminary training, which remained

---

14   Assistant Chief of Air Staff, "AAF Historical Studies: No. 1," 27.
15   Assistant Chief of Air Staff, "AAF Historical Studies: No. l," 33.

essentially the same, were Class B students. Class B graduates of the Preliminary course and Class A students entered the thirty-hour Elementary training. It was similar to the previously offered Preliminary course for Class A students, with one exception: the new course focused on officer preparation. The thirty hours were split between dual and solo flights:

| Dual flight | 13.5 hours |
| Solo flight | 16.5 hours |

Of these hours, five had to be night landings conducted from 500, 800, and 1,000 feet.[16]

The ground school which accompanied this phase consisted of a total of 117 hours. It was broken down into the following segments:

Military training	24 hours
Ground training	55 hours
Medical training	11 hours
Physical training	24 hours
Line maintenance	3 hours[17]

The third phase in training was Basic. It was open to only graduates of Elementary training and consisted of both dual and solo training.

---

16 Assistant Chief of Air Staff, "AAF Historical Studies: No. 1," 30-31.
17 Assistant Chief of Air Staff, "AAF Historical Studies: No. 1," 41.

	Dual	Solo
Familiarization	2 hours	
Precision landings, basic maneuvers, and precision flying	5 hours	8 hours
Soaring	1 hour	
Night flying	2 hours	4 hours
Navigational flights and strange field landings	2 hours	4 hours

It also included ten hours in a Link Trainer and at least three passenger hours in a tow ship.[18]

The Basic ground school totaled 106 ground hours, divided in the following manner:

Military	24 hours
Ground	46 hours
Medical	9 hours
Physical	24 hours
Line maintenance	3 hours[19]

The final stage of training was the Advanced phase. The original forty-hour plan was revised to fifteen hours. These hours covered the following:

---

18 Assistant Chief of Air Staff, "AAF Historical Studies: No. 1," 41.
19 Assistant Chief of Air Staff, "AAF Historical Studies: No. 1," 41.

	Dual	Solo
Familiarization flight tow	1/2 hour	
Tow technique, takeoff, climb, climbing turns, straight and level tows, recovery from bad tow position, including prop wash	1 hour	1 hour
Coordination exercises	1/2 hour	1/2 hour
Stalls, partial and complete, with immediate recovery from straight glides and gliding turns	1 hour	1 hour
Precision flying	1 hour	1 hour
Landings, including use of brakes and nose skid for short roll	1 hour	1 hour
Accuracy landings		1 hour
Descent on tow from 3,000 feet to 180° side position	1/2 hour	1/2 hour
Night flying	1 hour	2 hours
Final check		1/2 hour

The final five hours of daytime flying and the last hour of night flight was to be flown with a full cargo load.[20] Unfortunately, this was not always done, and there were cases of pilots entering combat carrying a gross load for the first time.

The Advanced ground school training totaled twenty-five hours, broken down as follows:

---

20 Assistant Chief of Air Staff, "AAF Historical Studies: No. 1," 43.

Maintenance of gliders and tow equipment	10 hours
Tactical maps and aerial projections	5 hours
Aircraft identification	6 hours
Camouflage	2 hours
Maintenance, lashing in, and operation of jeeps in glider mockups	2 hours[21]

The structural failure of the fifteen-place glider led to a revision of the Advanced training curriculum. On December 21, 1942, the total training hours were reduced from fifteen hours to eight hours.

> It would appear that this directive was arbitrarily promulgated without proper consultation of those men fully grounded in the needs and methods of glider training. Examination of the program of instruction ... reveals that the time provided for flying training was entirely inadequate.[22]

The report goes on to state,

> It was felt throughout the entire Flying Training Command that a candidate could not learn to fly a CG-4A glider efficiently in eight hours. Advanced schools were forced to graduate men who were not fully qualified glider pilots, and during the two months that this directive was in effect, dissatisfaction and disillusionment were rife among the instructor personnel.[23]

The Advanced training revisions reduced the program to the following:

---

21 Assistant Chief of Air Staff, "AAF Historical Studies: No. 1," 43.
22 Assistant Chief of Air Staff, "AAF Historical Studies: No. 1," 49.
23 Assistant Chief of Air Staff, "AAF Historical Studies: No. 1," 49.

	Dual	Solo
Day transition	3 hours	3 hours
Night flying	1 hour	1 hour
Copilot/passenger time	7 hours	

It was further prescribed that "students requiring more than four hours dual should be eliminated."[24]

The continued reduction in glider trainees brought on by the reduced quota relieved the situation. On February 27, 1943, the Advanced training program was reinstated at fifteen hours.

	Dual	Solo
Flying training:		
Day	5:30	6:30
Night	1:00	2:00
Broken down, the flying training included:		
Takeoffs and landings	1:00	1:00
Air work (high tow)[25]	1:00	1:00
Traffic patterns and landings	1:00	3:00
Descent on tow	1:00	1:00

---

24 FTC Memorandum No. 50-1-1, Feb. 1, 1943, quoted by Assistant Chief of Air Staff, "AAF Historical Studies: No. 1," 49.

25 High tow meant working above the towplane while still attached by a towrope. On low tow the glider was either level with the towplane or below it. Mousseau, interview, 20 June 1989.

Navigation training		2:00
Formation flying	0:30	0:30
Proficiency check	1:00	1:00[26]

Still, the training was considered all too brief. Ground school training hours had also increased to 105 hours. They were broken down as follows:

Military	24 hours
Ground	47 hours
Physical	24 hours
Line maintenance	10 hours[27]

One final rendition of the Advanced training program took place. On August 16, 1943, it was increased to twenty-five hours, and special emphasis was placed on tactical landings. They were accomplished by fully loaded gliders landing in fields with hurdles in them. The increased hours were also used to practice double towing, which was used on a few combat missions.

	Dual	Solo
Transition to CG-4As	2 hours	3 hours
Tactical type landings	2:30 hours	5:30 hours

---

26 Assistant Chief of Air Staff, "AAF Historical Studies: No. 1," 68-69.
27 Assistant Chief of Air Staff, "AAF Historical Studies: No. 1," 70.

Night flying (formation and landings)	2 hours	4 hours
Double tow (simulated small field landings)	1 hour	
Formation and tactical landings (over obstacles)	1 hour	1 hour
Contour cross-country (maximum altitude 200 feet)		2 hours
Proficiency check	1 hour	
Instrument (Link Trainer)	5 hours[28]	

---

28   Assistant Chief of Air Staff, "AAF Historical Studies: No. 1," 73.

www.ingramcontent.com/pod-product-compliance
Lightning Source LLC
LaVergne TN
LVHW041941070526
838199LV00051BA/2869